SPIRITUALITY
ROOTED IN
LITURGY

SHAWN
MADIGAN

The Pastoral Press

Washington, DC

ISBN: 0-912405-56-2

© 1988 The Pastoral Press

The Pastoral Press
225 Sheridan Street, NW
Washington, DC 20011
(202) 723-1254

The Pastoral Press is the publications division of the National Association of Pastoral Musicians, a membership organization of musicians and clergy dedicated to fostering the art of musical liturgy.
Printed in the United States of America.

CONTENTS

LIST OF ABBREVIATIONS

Acta = *Acta Synodalia Sacrosancti Concilii Oecumenici Vaticani Secundi*

GS = *Gaudium et Spes,* The Constitution on the Church in the Modern World

LG = *Lumen Gentium,* The Constitution on the Church

PG = Migne, *Patrologia Graeca*

PL = Migne, *Patrologia Latina*

SC = *Sacrosanctum Concilium,* The Constitution on the Sacred Liturgy

INTRODUCTION

LITURGICAL SPIRITUALITY IS THE TRADITIONAL ECCLESIAL MODEL OF CHRIS-
tian spiritual direction. In this age of cultural and ecclesial religious renewal, private spiritual direction is still more popular than
liturgical spiritual direction. The reasons for this may be both
cultural and ecclesial.

The "American way" is notoriously individualistic. A more
privatized spirituality is a natural theological outgrowth of that
cultural perspective. From an ecclesial standpoint, Vatican II
returned to an emphasis on the "people of God," a foundational
concept for renewal of ecclesial and liturgical life. Ritual reforms
of liturgy necessarily accompanied that emphasis on a community
expressed and formed in the paschal mystery. But the dangerous
nature of "proclaiming the death of the Lord until he comes" is
only beginning to be realized by the majority of Christian communities.

Is it possible for American Christians to enter a communal
memory, when that may mean death to some forms of life, liberty,
and pursuit of happiness? Is it possible for an ecclesial community
of laity and hierarchy to proclaim, and so to become, mutual jour-
neyers and creators of the incarnational meanings of the new
creation in Christ? A certain defensive amnesia is understandable
when the Christian memory that is past, present, and future,
claims the new creation will have no more barriers between rich
and poor, enslaved and free, male and female, titled and untitled,
powerful and powerless, clergy and laity.

To celebrate the death of the Lord until he comes is to celebrate
the mysticism of liturgical spirituality. The heart of that spirituality
is Jesus Christ, whose liturgy brings the world's liturgy into the
realm of graciousness. The Christian assurance of a new and eter-

nal covenant bears testimony to the new heaven and the new earth that are part of the Christian dream, and the best of the American dream. The communal nature of these complementary dreams, imaged in the body of Christ, reflects and contains those human hopes that are essential to the drama of the unfolding history of all times and places.

To proclaim the death of the Lord until he comes is to proclaim the infinity and intimacy of the Christian memory. The infinity of the memory points to one perspective of liturgical spirituality. The intimacy of the memory points to another. There is a humanly incomprehensible epiphany of the Lord which embraces the world's biography of past, present, and future. There is also an intimacy of the memory. It is this experience which challenges the conscious proclaimers of the new creation to incarnationalize the memory, regardless of the structural changes and costs necessary to mediate the meaning.

The danger of the Christian memory is that it includes myriad forms of death as well as life. The paschal question at the heart of liturgical spirituality challenges the communities of believers in every age. How do we answer the paschal question, "What must legitimately die and what must be transformed to more effectively proclaim the death of the Lord until he comes in glory?" Ongoing revisions in understanding will bring forms of death but also of life to persons, communities, and the church universal. Every revision manifests the death and resurrection inherent in the ongoing creation of a new heaven and a new earth.

This work cannot adequately answer the paschal question for this age. It can point to some foundational understandings of liturgical spirituality that make the question more comprehensible. The simple purpose of this work is to introduce basic concepts of and possibilities for Christian liturgical spirituality. To accomplish that purpose, the following procedure will be used.

Foundational concepts of liturgical spirituality will be generally described, defined, and compared to other concepts of Christian spirituality (Ch.1). A necessarily selective, and so partial, historical development of liturgical spirituality will be presented (Ch. 2-5). Some contemporary cultural and ecclesial issues that raise questions about the future of liturgical spirituality will be set forth (Ch.6-8). A final chapter will focus some issues of liturgical spirituality that flow from the growing house church movement, a movement that has assumed global proportions in this twentieth century. The potential renewal of liturgical life that is still to come will only be hinted at throughout the text. That topic could well be the topic for future volumes.

For whom is this work intended? In general, it is intended for any reflective Christian who senses a mysticism inherent in proclaiming the death of the Lord until he comes. In particular, the work is intended for those whose lives have been, are, or will be, involved in some form of liturgical ministry. The end of each chapter contains further thematic reflections and basic resources to develop the issues that are merely introduced in the chapters. Any professor of liturgy will readily adapt, amplify, and enrich these reflections and the resources suggested.

As with any work of this sort, there are people whose help facilitated the completion of the text. The following professional liturgists took time from overcommitted schedules to respond to sections of the text, namely, David N. Power, O.M.I., Gail Ramshaw, Mark Searle, R. Kevin Seasoltz, O.S.B., Gerard Sloyan, Janet Walton, and Will Willimon. Family members, my mother Grace, brother John, and sister-in-law Kathleen, cheered the efforts on to completion, while Linda Taylor, C.S.J., undertook the tedious task of proofreading. Larry Johnson, Director of The Pastoral Press, guided the work from manuscript to printed form. A grant from the Bush Foundation, provided through the College of Saint Catherine, enabled research time and writing time over the summer months. Thanks are due to the graciousness of all these people and foundations.

If this work facilitates the reader's appreciation of the liturgical spirituality that makes the epiphany of the Lord in all of life more "real," it is worthwhile. If in addition, it encourages anyone to risk deeper entrance into the fascinating danger of proclaiming the death of the Lord until he comes, it will have attained a graciousness that is beyond human power to effect.

Feast of the Epiphany, 1988

ONE

CHRISTIAN SPIRITUALITY, A LITURGICAL SPIRITUALITY

To know Christ and the power of his resurrection
(Phil 3:10)

CHRISTIAN SPIRITUALITY IS AN INCARNATIONAL AND ECCLESIAL SPIRITU-
ality, whose source of meaning and life is Jesus Christ. Christian
spirituality is a future oriented spirituality, for the resurrection of
Jesus Christ is a mystery that points to the future. The fullness of the
paschal mystery, the life, death, and resurrection of Christ, is a new
creation. The newness has begun. "God has given us the wisdom to
understand fully the mystery, the plan he was pleased to decree in
Christ, to be carried out in the fullness of time." (Eph 1:9-10)
    For Christians it is Jesus Christ who is the model of holiness.
"Let us keep our eyes fixed on Jesus, who inspires and perfects
our faith. For the sake of the joy which lay before him, he endured
the cross ... He has taken his place at the right hand of God."
(Heb 12:2-3). The holiness to which Christians are called is both
personal and communal. Those who are personally united with
Jesus Christ enter into the universal horizons of his love.

> By his incarnation, the Son of God has united himself in some
> fashion with everyone. Christ died for all. We ought to believe that
> the Holy Spirit, in a manner known only to God, offers to everyone
> the possibility of being associated with this paschal mystery.[1]

1. GS 22. In Walter Abbott, ed., *The Documents of Vatican II* (Chicago:
Follett, 1966) 221-22.

The paschal mystery of Jesus Christ is the central mystery celebrated by the church. The celebration is both expressive and formative of the community. Each day, each week, each season of the church year, the paschal mystery remains as the foundational memory from which the ongoing Christian story is created. New stories will be expressive of the transforming power. But always the same context will frame the meaning of the story. "Lord, by your cross and resurrection, you have set us free. You are the Savior of the world." (Eucharistic Acclamation D)

All Christian spirituality is formed from this mystery and leads to the mystery. The mystery, Christ manifest through his Body, the church, makes Christian spirituality an essentially communal spirituality. From the beginning of his teaching Jesus made the community nature of his mission clear. Discipleship was a public reality as well as a personal response. The twelve, symbols of the new Israel, are gathered from many different backgrounds. They and all disciples shall be sent to gather the lost, the sick, and the poor as a sign of the presence of the new age of God's reign. The community is called to be salt for the earth and light for the world. As a leaven is used to form new dough, so the community shall be used to point to the way all people are meant to live in the covenant mystery of God. The power of the resurrection reaches the world through this new creation. The community is the Body that is given for all.[2]

Christian spirituality originates, and is constantly renewed, through the liturgical celebration of the mystery. Liturgy is "the summit toward which the activity of the church is directed" and "the fountain from which all her power flows."[3] The liturgical life of the church provides a daily, weekly, and seasonal environment for spiritual direction of the Christian community. Ritualized moments of the Christian life focus the meaning of personal journeying within the pilgrim community. Thus the liturgical life of the church, accenting seasonal rhythms of the paschal mystery, provides an environment that embraces the dying and rising in every life.

Liturgy celebrates the presence of Christ for all people. Chris-

2. Gerhard Lohfink, *Jesus and Community: The Social Dimension of Christian Faith* (Philadelphia: Fortress Press, 1984) 63-73.
3. SC 10; Abbott, *The Documents* 142.

tians proclaim that universality whenever they proclaim Christ. "You are the Savior of the world!" The public prayer of the community manifests the hoped for kingdom to which all are called. The loving presence of Christ, consciously known by the gathered community, touches the hearts of multitudes beyond the gathered community.

But the Christian community is graced to know the rhythmic memory of Christ who is always present to those who remember. All Christian spirituality is based upon remembering, especially remembering the paschal mystery that is foundational to the church. As life unfolds in daily, weekly, and yearly accents for remembering, so the liturgical life of the church in Christ unfolds in daily, weekly, and yearly rhythms.

> Christ is always present in his church, especially in her liturgical celebrations . . . Every week, on the day she has called the Lord's Day, she keeps the memory of his resurrection . . . Within the cycle of a year, she unfolds the whole mystery of Christ . . . the purpose of the Office is to sanctify the day.[4]

Though Christian communal prayer has its foundation in the public prayer of the church, Christian prayer is not confined to this expression. The paschal mystery of Jesus Christ may be experienced through varieties of life situations, and unique modes of prayer that flow from life experiences. The history of Christian spirituality reflects many ways of coming to know Jesus Christ and the power of his resurrection. When coming to know Christ has a structured set of disciplines, modes of prayer, and basic expectations of disciples, then schools of spirituality may arise. The purpose of any school of spirituality is to liberate its disciples for greater love of the Lord and his people.

SCHOOLS OF SPIRITUALITY: METHODS FOR LIBERATION

Schools of spirituality structure a life environment that serves as a method for liberation. The challenge to lifelong conversion of heart is facilitated by the lifestyle of the particular school of spirituality. History reflects a rich variety of such schools. Each

4. SC 7, 102, 88; Abbott, *The Documents* 140-41, 168, 164.

school resembles others in its intent to know Christ Jesus and the power of his resurrection. Each school resembles others in its seriousness of response to some basic Christian questions. "Who do you say that I am?" (Mk 8:32) "Do you understand what I have done for you?" (Jn 13:12) "Have I been so long with you and still you do not know me?" (Jn 14:9) "Do you love me?" (Jn 21:16)

Schools of spirituality differ from each other in their mode of responding to the questions. Certain emphases of the gospel will be stressed in each school which are not stressed in the same way by other schools. Schools of spirituality will have a preferred image of Jesus Christ, which in turn affects the theology of the church that is preferred as well as a Christian anthropology. Certain ascetical practices, modes of prayer, service, and kind of community life will flow from the religious imagination that is the basis for the school.

Schools of spirituality may be named according to a culture within which they arose. Schools may also be named after a founder or other person significant in forming or renewing its spirituality. History reflects a rich variety of schools of spirituality. Some lasted for a long period of time, whereas others were significant for lesser periods of time. A brief description of some schools of spirituality may illustrate the differences that can occur when comparing schools.

The Russian school of spirituality is named after the culture which is foundational to its experience of Jesus Christ. The image of Jesus Christ favored by the Russian school is a kenotic Christ. This Christ "emptied himself and took the form of a slave ... humbled himself, obediently accepting even death, death on a cross!" (Phil 2:7-8) The Russian school emphasizes the suffering Christ, the humiliated Christ who did not complain, but silently endured. Through his suffering and because of his obedience, "God highly exalted him and bestowed on him a name above every other name." (Phil 2:9) The tradition of discipleship that grew out of this image stressed gentle suffering. The patient endurance of this suffering will bring a reward of peace and exultation. The history of the people of Russia suggests why this interpretation of Christ and the paschal mystery is a meaningful one. If history is to be a source of hope rather than despair, the suffering that is part of that history must have some image of hope for the future. Following Christ by patient endurance will eventually bring resurrection. One commentator summarizes the richness and complexity of the Russian school of spirituality in this way.

> The Russian church has especially loved and venerated a tradition of gentle sufferers, a feeling complemented by the power of belief in the resurrection and its universal application.[5]

The Franciscan school of spirituality favors a kenotic image of Christ also. But the image is given a slightly different interpretation and application. For Francis of Assisi, the founder of this school, the kenotic Christ was one who did not cling to anything, even a self-image as God. In imitation of Christ, early Franciscans chose a radical poverty as a means for knowing the Christ who emptied himself. The Franciscan tradition has a history of varied interpretations and understandings of the poverty of Christ reflected in communal poverty. But for all Franciscans, a freely chosen poverty is more Christological and evangelical than disciplinary. The poverty of Franciscans, like the poverty of Christ, is a means of relating to all creation. Only those who do not cling possessively to people, to things, to their own importance, and even to the beauties of the earth, can appreciate the inherent value of the world. That spirit of kenosis will mediate knowing Christ whose presence is manifest through all creation.[6]

A different preferred image of Jesus Christ appears in the Jesuit tradition. This tradition is named after the community known as the Society of Jesus. Jesus Christ is imaged as an intimate friend, a servant of the Father who does all for the glory of the Father. The faith of Christ is the model for the discernment question that characterizes Jesuit spirituality. "What will most likely lead to the greater honor and glory of God?"[7] The universality of service that characterized the love of Jesus Christ provides a paradigm for the universal apostolate of the Jesuits. Whatever will lead to the greater honor and glory of God can be undertaken. The willing-

5. Robin Aizlewood, "Russian Spirituality," in *The Westminster Dictionary of Christian Spirituality*, ed. Gordon S. Wakefield (Philadelphia: Westminster Press, 1983) 342.
6. Eric Doyle, "Franciscan Spirituality," in *The Westminster Dictionary of Christian Spirituality* 159-61.
7. George E. Ganss, "Society of Jesus," in *The Westminster Dictionary of Christian Spirituality* 224-26.

ness to risk attempting whatever is asked is a sign of humility in this tradition. Humility knows that it is always the Lord's power that "can do immeasurably more than we can ask or imagine." (Eph 3:20) The emphasis on service that is central to Jesuit spirituality affects the other aspects of spiritual life. The mode of communal prayer, asceticism, and action encourages a spirituality of contemplation in action.[8]

Benedictine spirituality, named after the sixth century founder, emphasizes a Christ image of compassion and gentleness. Community life is a source of inherent asceticism, of liberation of heart, and of the realization that the love of God is given tangible expression in the love and forgiveness essential to community life. Habitual attention to the Word of God is fostered through the life setting in the monastery as a school of discipleship. The Word of God is mediated through scripture or other books meditatively read (lectio divina). The work of God, the communal liturgy of the eucharist and of the hours, provides a prayerful setting for the other works of God, or ministries. Through the silence that fosters a listening heart, each attends to the Lord. The Rule of Benedict sees the abbot or abbess as a kind of sacrament of Christ. Ideally, one's relationship to God is given tangible expression in the love, trust, and obedience which binds abbess or abbot to each member of the community. The approximately fourteen centuries of Benedictine spirituality have witnessed many movements, variations, and particular styles of interpretations. Both the chronological appearance and the basic understanding of human weaknesses and strengths make this spirituality a foundational basis for other Christian spiritualities.[9]

These brief summaries of some schools of spirituality do not reflect the historical pluralities of expressions and interpretations that evolved within the schools. As history progresses, any school of spirituality will interpret anew what its dominant Christ image means. Historical circumstances may affect the rise or fall of popularity of the schools. Renewal movements within the church, within society, or within the schools themselves may bring new

8. Hugo Rahner, "The Christology of the Spiritual Exercises," *Ignatius the Theologian* (New York: Herder and Herder, 1968) 53-135.
9. Maria Boulding, "Benedictine Spirituality, Benedictines," in *The Westminster Dictionary of Christian Spirituality* 41-42.

interpretations of meanings. Such renewed interpretations may seem to some to be destroying or ignoring earlier meanings. For others, renewed interpretation is the source of continuity of the tradition. The spirit, rather than the expression of a tradition, provides continuity in any school. If there are severe differences about which expressions best retain the original intent of the school, different groups may emerge within the same tradition. This has happened many times in the history of Christian spirituality.

As brief as this description is, it does point to a small sample of the richness of the Christian tradition and the many ways there are of living into the paschal mystery. Schools of spirituality provide a structured life setting that encourages lifelong growth in response to the gospel. Some Christians choose a particular school that seems appropriate to their experience of Christ and the mode of liberation they require. Other Christians do not consciously choose a school of spirituality but live within the liturgical school of spirituality that is shared by all Christians.

LITURGY: THE CHURCH'S SCHOOL OF SPIRITUALITY

The liturgy can be called the school of spirituality that is formative and expressive of the church, the people of God. In this school there is not one preferred image of Christ, but rather many images of Christ. These images flow from the paschal mystery of Jesus Christ. That mystery and its meanings unfold through the course of the liturgical year.

> Within the cycle of a year, the church unfolds the whole mystery of Christ . . . opens to the faithful the riches of her Lord's powers and mercies, so that these are in some way made present at all times, and the faithful are enabled to lay hold of them.[10]

There is a call to discipleship that the paschal mystery affirms, proclaiming that Christian holiness is imaged in the universality of love manifest through the community. The holiness of the church is seen by the measure of its concern for itself and its concern for world transformation. The liturgical prayer of the church

10. SC 102; Abbott, *The Documents* 68.

7

provides a focus for liturgical spirituality. Liturgical prayer, prayer in union with Christ, is both prayer and action for the world. Prayer in union with Christ is always universal, for Jesus Christ "joins the entire community of humanity to himself, associating it with his own singing of the canticle of divine praise."[11]

Whatever a Christian does in the name of Christ has some effect on humanity. Whether it is formal prayer, work, or other action, all life lived in union with Christ becomes a song of praise. This was the thought behind the command to pray always. "Rejoice always, never cease praying, render constant thanks; such is God's will for you in Christ Jesus." (2 Thes 5:16-18)

The New Testament points to the relationship of liturgical prayer and liturgical spirituality. To "never cease praying" meant to do all in the name of Jesus Christ, in union with him. "Leitourgia," liturgy, incorporated cultic liturgy and life's liturgy. Cultic duty, works of love, and even death itself are all "leitourgia" (Lk 1:23; Heb 8:65; 2 Cor 9:12; Phil 9:30).[12] Early Christian writers had a clear sense that liturgy referred to all of life, for Jesus Christ was the source of reconciliation of all creation and sanctification.

Jesus Christ, by his most merciful coming has consecrated the whole world. The church, by her sacramental rites, renews this consecration . . . everything is directed toward the mystery of the Lord.[13]

The essential integrity between cultic liturgy, or prayer of the church, and life's liturgy was one way of explaining how Christians could pray without ceasing. Origen in his treatise on prayer comments on the integrity of cultic prayer and life.

The one who links together prayer with deeds of duty and fits seemly actions with that prayer is the one who prays without ceas-

11. SC 83; Abbott, *The Documents* 163.
12. William E. Willimon, *Worship as Pastoral Care* (Nashville: Abingdon, 1982) 15-30, 41-48.
13. Gabriel M. Brasso, *Liturgy and Spirituality* (Collegeville: The Liturgical Press, 1971) 16.

ing; for the virtuous, deeds are taken up as part of prayer ... The whole life of the saint is one mighty, integrated prayer.[14]

A liturgical spirituality, like other schools of spirituality, includes ascetical practices. But these practices grow out of the particular season of the church year and what it reveals of the paschal mystery of Jesus Christ. The rhythm of the daily, the weekly, and the yearly are focused in the life, death, and resurrection of Christ. The prayer of the church in every season points to the social nature of salvation and liberation in Christ. This does not diminish the personal nature of liturgical prayer, but it does invite everyone to enter into the mystery of the intimacy and infinity of the love of Christ.

> We turn toward each other, and outward to all people, not by abandoning the personal journey but precisely as part of it ... If there is no personal depth that comes from one's journey into the God within each of us, then neither the eucharist, nor the sacraments, nor the liturgy of the hours can be considered true prayer.[15]

However, there is a difference in content between liturgical prayer and the prayer of solitude. Liturgical prayer, or prayer of the church, invites the community to enter into the intimacy and universality of the love of Christ. The prayer of solitude, or prayer of the heart, is an individual's unique experience of the paschal mystery. Liturgical spirituality includes both modes of prayer, for liturgical spirituality embraces all of life lived in Christ. It may be helpful to clarify the differences between the two basic forms of prayer that can be expressive as well as formative of liturgical spirituality.

CHRISTIAN PRAYER: ECCLESIAL AND SOLITARY

The liturgical prayer of the church and the solitary prayer of the heart are two expressions of the Christian experience of the

14. Origen, *Treatise on Prayer*, trans. E. G. Jay (London: SPCK, 1954) XII.2.
15. Peter E. Fink, "Public and Private Moments in Christian Prayer," *Worship* 58:6 (November 1984) 492-93.

paschal mystery. As life rhythms include communal and solitary moments, so the rhythm of prayer will include communal and private expressions. Always, the source of the prayer will be the same. "No one can say 'Jesus is Lord' unless it is under the influence of the Spirit". (1 Cor 12:3) Regardless of the form of prayer, whenever a Christian prays, the act itself is a declaration that Jesus is Lord.

The prayer of the church and the unique prayer of the heart complement each other. The prayer of the heart, in its varied forms of expression, should "harmonize with the liturgical seasons, accord with the sacred liturgy," and "lead the people to it."[16] The prayer of the church can provide a larger context of community that may call individuals to a greater need for prayer of solitude so that one can be liberated for the creative love conducive to community. The journey into the paschal mystery is the end of all forms of prayer, but the "the liturgy by its very nature far surpasses any of them."[17]

No one can pierce the way through to the silent liturgy of the heart without first having shared in celebrating the visible liturgy of the church.[18]

The visible liturgy of the church is prayer in the name of all humanity redeemed in Christ. "Father, you are holy indeed and all creation rightly gives you praise." (Eucharistic Prayer III) The gathered church, the body of Christ, remembers the horizon of love the community is called to live. The blood of the new and everlasting covenant is shed "for you and for all so that sins may be forgiven." The community is empowered to transform the earth, for they are what they receive, "The Body of Christ. Amen."

The silent liturgy of the heart, the prayer of solitude, has a different focus. The contours of one's unique life provide a unique setting within which the paschal mystery unfolds. The mystery is one, but the individuals who experience and embody the mystery

16. SC 13; Abbott, *The Documents* 143.
17. SC 13; Abbott, *The Documents* 143.
18. André Louf, *Teach Us to Pray*, trans. H. Hoskins (Chicago: Franciscan Herald Press, 1975) 94.

are unique individuals. The meaning of the mystery unfolds in the life of each person in a unique way. Prayer of the heart is as unique as the person who reflects on the meaning of life in Christ.

> For there are as many kinds of prayer as there are states and conditions of any soul, of every spiritual being. I think that all the different kinds of prayer cannot be understood without great purity of heart and soul, and the light of the Holy Spirit.[19]

In the course of Christian history, many guides have devised models for the prayer of the heart. These models are intended to facilitate prayer. If a method is needed to liberate the ability or willingness to follow the Spirit, the method should be appropriate to the person. Method is not prayer, nor is it an end in itself. It should be used only to the degree it is necessary. The great spiritual writers have all been well aware of the mystery that God alone leads each person to love, and so to pray, in a manner appropriate to that person.

> It will sometimes happen that immediately after the preparation, you will feel your affections moved toward God. In this case, yield to the attractions. Let them have their free course whenever they are present.[20]

In spite of the necessary uniqueness of both content and form of the solitary prayer of the heart, it is ordered to community. Prayer is the renewing preoccupation with Jesus Christ, and the preoccupation of Jesus Christ, "especially his concern for humanity," is the hallmark of Christian prayer and mysticism.[21]

It has long been a tradition of Christian prayer that "the rightful door leading to contemplation is love."[22] The paschal mystery of

19. John Cassian, "Collationes," PL 49: 781.

20. Francis de Sales, *Introduction to the Devout Life* (New York: World Publishing Co., 1952) II.8, p.97.

21. Francis Martin, "The Humanity of Christian Mysticism," *Cross Currents* XXIV (Summer-Fall 1974) 234.

22. St. Isaac the Syrian, "Directions on Spiritual Training," trans. E. Kadloubovsky and G. E. Palmer, *Philokalia: Early Fathers from the Philokalia* (London: Faber and Faber, 1954) 197.

Jesus Christ provides a horizon of universality for that love. A measure of prayer is the measure of love for all.

> Our Lord Jesus Christ suffered for the whole of mankind and gave equally to all the hope of resurrection ... If you hate some, neither love nor hate others, love some moderately, but others very intensely, then learn from the unequalness that you are far from perfect love, which enjoins equal love for all.[23]

The liturgy of the church and the liturgy of the heart exist as complements in the life environment of liturgical spirituality. If all of life is liturgy, an occasion of praise and thanks, then all modes of prayer and action can mediate the awareness of the Risen Christ and the power of his resurrection. There is a difference not only in the content of the prayer of the church and the prayer of the heart, but also in the context of each.

The context for the prayer of the church is a community gathered together to enter the paschal mystery of Jesus Christ. The response to the call of Christ to be world transformers is a response made within and by the community. The context for the the prayer of the heart is one of solitude before the Lord, the experience of the uniqueness of one's life lived in Christ.

These basic samenesses and differences in the two modes of Christian prayer provide a foundation for considering two modes of spiritual direction. The uniqueness of one's life in the Lord can be a reason for seeking private spiritual direction. The Christian community's life in the Lord is guided by liturgical spiritual direction. Both forms of spiritual direction are prevalent in the history of the church, with a wide variety of expressions. The next section will briefly identify the general samenesses and differences between the two forms of spiritual direction.

TWO MODELS OF LIFE DIRECTION: PRIVATE
AND LITURGICAL

Models of spiritual direction, like models of prayer, share some commonalities. All models of spiritual direction or life direction share the same purpose. Each has a method that leads to the ac-

23. St. Maximus the Confessor, "Centuries on Love," *Philokalia* 197.

complishment of that purpose. There is a relationship of persons in each model and a presumption of some continuity in the process. But the way that these commonalities function is different in the models of direction.

Private Model of Life Direction

The private model of life direction is concerned with the uniqueness of a person who has felt the call toward deeper conversion in Christ. A director is sought to aid in the discernment process. Ideally, the director will have a trained sensitivity to the myriad rhythms of conversion, greater life experience, and deeper prayer experience than the person to be guided. The director must also have a disciplined awareness of personal strengths and weaknesses, so that there can be a non-biased listening to the experience of another.

There is a mutuality involved in the process of direction as one person entrusts portions of life to another. Questions can be a means of discernment. How has the call to conversion come? Has it come through vocational doubts, loneliness, a disorienting experience of love, death, justice, compassion, or shattered individualism? Can the individual seeking a deeper union with the Lord identify the forms of entombment that are preventing new life? As the director and the individual being guided engage in the process, a clarity about the relationship of director and directee needs to be set forth.

Will the relationship be that of mentor to one with less life experience? Will the relationship be one of mutual discernment as friends in the Lord, or of spiritual mother or father to daughter or son? Will the relationship be one of friends who share all of life, and discernment be one aspect of that sharing? Or will discernment of one aiding another be the only context for relationship in the Lord? It is important to set forth such expectations at the beginning of the process, so that the relationship remains a help rather than a hindrance.[24]

A method to facilitate the process of prayerful discernment will

24. James Gau, "Relationships in Spiritual Direction," in *Spiritual Direction: Contemporary Readings,* ed. Kevin Culligan, O.C.D. (New York: Living Flame Press, 1983) 83-97.

be decided upon. The purpose for seeking guidance, the type person who seeks the guidance, the present vocational context of the person, and other factors influence which methods are appropriate to the life setting. Ultimately, a method must liberate the person to enter the solitary space in which the Lord is met in a unique way. Then the questions that arise from that unique and creative intimacy will be given some answer. The answer may be partial, because the questions are still partial. But, as Moche tells Eliezar in *Night:*

> There are a thousand and one gates leading into the orchard of mystical truth. Every human being has his own gate. We must never make the mistake of wanting to enter the orchard by any gate but our own.[25]

The continuity of the process of life direction is necessary if the rhythms of conversion are to be sources for enlightenment. As the rhythms of conversion are apparent, there may be need to adjust or change methods. A time may also come when an individual is able to listen, interpret, and follow the movements of the Spirit without the aid of another. At that point, life direction by another may not be necessary. The liturgical life of the church may suffice as the model of spiritual direction that is most appropriate at that time.

Liturgical Model of Life Direction

"For centuries, the liturgy, actively celebrated, has been the most important form of pastoral care."[26] Pastoral care, the awareness of the love of Jesus Christ as well as the challenge that love brings, was linked to the liturgy by Vatican II. The liturgy "is the outstanding means by which the faithful can express in their lives, and manifest to others, the mystery of Christ and the real nature of the true Church."[27]

25. Advice given by Moche to Eliezar in Elie Wiesel, *Night* (New York: Avon Books, 1969) 14.
26. J. A. Jungmann, *Pastoral Liturgy* (New York: Herder and Herder, 1962) 380.
27. SC 2; Abbott, *The Documents* 137.

The community, rather than unique individuals, is the subject of liturgical spiritual direction. The measure of the community's conversion in Christ is the degree of universality of love manifest through its life of prayer and mission.

The liturgical model of life direction calls the community to conversion. However, that does not mean that there is a lack of personal intimacy in the experience of Jesus Christ within the community. Universal love is not love in the abstract. It is a love manifest by those who have touched their own mystery of being loved in Christ. Knowing that love, they can extend that compassion beyond themselves, and in the process rediscover the mystery in ever new ways.

Cultic liturgy, the official communal celebration of the memory, challenges the community to experience the power of resurrection. The liturgy of life can manifest the proclamation of the cultic liturgy that Christ loves the world and is sent to free its people. The community is challenged to enter into the living memory of a life given "for you and for all." To enter into the mind and heart of Christ Jesus, the life of Christ, means to imitate the horizon of his love. Liturgy constantly invites the community to enter into, to express, and to continue the manifestation of the living memory. The confession of faith is a proclamation that is confirmed in manifestation of justice and love (1 Jn 2:29; 3:11-15).

The liturgy of the church provides the model of and for ongoing formation of the comunity into the paschal mystery of Jesus Christ. Everyone in the community is challenged to follow Christ. "All the faithful of Christ, of whatever rank or status are called to the fullness of the Christian life," for God calls each "according to His own purpose."[28]

The liturgical year unfolds the "whole mystery of Christ," so that the faithful can "lay hold of it and become filled with saving grace."[29] The liturgical year provides a continuity in the process of communal formation and direction. An abundance of images of Christ, of the meaning and mission of the Body of Christ, fills the seasons of the church year.

Regardless of the particular season, the paschal mystery remains focal. The relationship of Jesus Christ with and for the

28. LG 40; Abbott, *The Documents* 67.
29. SC 102; Abbott, *The Documents* 168.

human community is recalled whenever Christians eat the bread and drink the cup. In Advent the community prays as a symbol of the entire world. "The earth rejoices in hope of the Savior's coming, and looks forward with longing to his return at the end of time." (Third Sunday of Advent) At Christmas the community will again acknowledge the universality of the love of Christ. "He (Christ) has come to lift up all things to himself, to restore unity to creation, and to lead mankind from exile into your heavenly kingdom." (Christmas Preface II) At Easter "the joy of resurrection fills the whole world." (Easter Preface III) On Pentecost the community prays, "May the Spririt unite the races and nations on earth to proclaim your glory" and asks that the gospel "continue to work in the world through the hearts of all who believe." (Opening Prayer of the Vigil, and During the Day of Pentecost)

The paschal mystery is one of intimacy and infinity. The community that celebrates the intimacy of Christ must manifest the infinity of the love of Christ. The prayer of the church provides the contours of that intimacy and infinity. As the liturgical year unfolds the mystery of Jesus Christ, yesterday, today, and forever, there will be different emphases of the Word of the Lord. The prayer will focus a particular emphasis, for life lived in general may miss the necessary particularity of liberation. The seasons of the church year provide such accents or emphases of the paschal mystery.

But it is the Christian Sunday which provides the weekly discernment time for the Christian community. The unfolding of the paschal mystery has myriad shapes for the lifelong call to conversion of the heart. The prayers of the Sunday provide a wide variety of visions of the mystery of Christ reconciling the world and all its people to himself. "Open our eyes to see your hand at work in the beauty of creation, in the splendor of human life. Touched by your hand, our world is holy." (Seventeenth Sunday, Ordinary Time) "This is the night when Christians everywhere ... grow together in holiness. What good would life have been to us had Christ not come as our Redeemer?" (Easter Saturday Proclamation) "The love you offer always exceeds the furthest expression of our human longing, for you are greater than the human heart." (Third Sunday, Ordinary Time)

The liturgical model of life direction provides many sources that mediate the presence of Christ. The Word of the Lord, the homily, the community, the presider, and the whole order of Word and Sacrament mediate the presence of Christ.[30] In the liturgical model of life direction, the presider is not a private spiritual director, but rather a public person addressing a community who hears the Word in a communal setting, just as the presider does. The presider may be considered a chief discerner of the community gathered in Christ. This presumes that the presider has a sense of the heart of the community, at least insofar as it contains the heart of the presider in the common need for lifelong conversion to the Lord.

Both models of spiritual direction, private and liturgical, embrace the paschal mystery and enable liberating believers to grow more fully into that mystery. The liturgical action of the church is an action of Christ with this Body. "Every liturgical celebration, because it is an action of Christ the Priest and his Body, the Church, is a sacred action surpassing all others."[31] Liturgical spiritual direction may be complemented by private life direction. One can only enter into community according to the maturity of personal intimacy. The willingness to give those parts of individuality that must be given if community is to be formed in and with Christ is essential. Christian intimacy is ordered to building community that in turn functions to liberate the individual.

In summary, the two models of life direction are similar in their intent to challenge the community to lifelong conversion in Christ. Both present a means for knowing the power of Christ's resurrection. Each has its foundation in the paschal mystery, and intends to lead individuals and communities into the fullness of the mystery.

But there are also differences. Private spiritual or life direction starts with the individual in the solitude of the heart. Liturgical life direction begins with the community at the heart of the church. Private spiritual direction has another person facilitating the discernment of the particular call to conversion. Liturgical spiritual direction is an ecclesial mode of direction that is based in the liturgical life of the church. Private spiritual direction may have changing methods appropriate to the person being directed. Liturgical spiritual direction is a fixed manner of unfolding the

30. SC 10, 33; Abbott, *The Documents* 142, 149.
31. SC 7; Abbott, *The Documents* 141.

paschal mystery through time with the shape of conversion unfolding through the liturgical year. Finally, there may come a time when private life direction by another will no longer be necessary. There will never come a time when the liturgical life of the church will be considered unnecessary. Liturgy, "an action of Christ the Priest and his Body, the Church, is a sacred action surpassing all others."[32]

The liturgical life of the church and the liturgical prayer of the church are formative of and foundational for the Christian life. All expressions of Christian spirituality include this foundation. But parts of that foundation have provided the sources for many expressions of Christian spirituality throughout history. Thus, schools of spirituality have been, and will continue to be, created from this ecclesial source of life direction. Different images of Christ, different forms of prayer, different ascetical practices and modes of relationship to the world and its people, all contribute to the richness of Christian spirituality.

SUMMARY

This chapter has considered some introductory concepts and relationships that are operative in Christian spirituality. Christian spirituality is an incarnational, ecclesial, and liturgical spirituality. The foundation of Christian spirituality is the paschal mystery, the death and resurrection of Jesus Christ. The holiness of Jesus Christ is the model for Christian holiness and wholeness.

Christian holiness is based upon an incarnational mysticism, a life lived in Christ for the transformation of the world. The degree of personal relationship with Jesus Christ can be measured by the universal horizons of one's love for the world. The Body of Christ, the Christian community, can use a similar measure for its communal intimacy with Christ. Does the communal Body of Christ reflect the transubstantiation of its own life? Is it reflecting the power of the resurrection that reconciles all in Christ?

Liturgical spirituality is the ecclesial spirituality that focuses the mystery of the new creation in Christ. Though all of the Christian life is lived within and through the living memory of Christ, the liturgical life of the church gathers the community around and

32. SC 7; Abbott, *The Documents* 141.

into memory. The paschal mystery celebrated by the community at prayer is celebrated as well in the mission of the Christian community.

The mission of the Christian community in and for the world has a history of expression that includes varieties of schools of spirituality. Schools of spirituality structure a life environment that intends to liberate the disciples of that school for greater love of the Lord and his people. A preferred image of Christ, preferred emphases and interpretations of gospel living, and particular notions of ascetical practices, community, prayer, and ministry separate the different schools. At the same time, the paschal mystery and reconciliation of all in Christ provides a foundational sameness that is the starting point. The fullness of the paschal mystery, when Christ will be all in all, is a shared hope of all schools of spirituality.

Liturgical spirituality could be called the traditional school of Christian spirituality. It keeps the memory alive that is foundational to the Body of Christ. "Do this in memory of me." The liturgical life of the church embraces, continues, and manifests the memory through the transformation of all things in Christ. Liturgical spirituality, expressed in the liturgical life of the church, emphasizes the communal nature of Christian life and salvation. The universality of the love of Christ is the focal mystery that challenges the community to go beyond a privatized holiness into the inherent asceticism of communal holiness. The liturgical year unfolds the mystery of Christ through an abundance of images expressive of the mystery of the whole Christ, head and members.

Liturgical spirituality is focused through the liturgical prayer of the church. This communal prayer is ordered to transformation of the world into one community in Christ. Liturgical prayer is complemented by another mode of prayer, the prayer of solitude. The prayer of solitude expresses the silent liturgy of the heart, a liturgy that is unique to the life experiences and reflections of the one who prays. The purpose of the prayer of solitude is similar to the purpose of all Christian prayer, to liberate one to love as Christ loves. The content of the prayer of solitude will be as varied as the person who prays that prayer.

As there are two general modes of prayer, there are two general modes of spiritual or life direction, liturgical and private. Liturgical life direction is an ecclesial direction of the Christian community into the mystery of Christ. Private spiritual direction is direction of the individual toward the mystery of Christ. The intent of both modes of spiritual direction is similar. The content and context of the modes of direction differ. Each mode of life direction can complement the other. Private spiritual direction may be more or less necessary for an individual as life progresses, but liturgical spiritual direction will remain integral for the Christian community in its journey toward the fullness of the resurrection.

The foundational nature of liturgical spiritual direction in the life of the Christian community may be better understood through the filter of its past. Early Christian liturgical spirituality grew out of certain reinterpretations of Jewish liturgical spirituality. Jewish liturgical spirituality was formative of Jesus Christ and his contemporaries. In context of that spirituality, the Christian memory was something old and something new.

FURTHER THEMATIC DEVELOPMENT

1. Compare the content and form of the liturgical prayers of the church for a major feast, for example, All Saints, Christmas, Easter, Ascension, Pentecost, and so on, to the content and form of a collection of prayers of solitude.

SOME SOURCES

The Sacramentary; The Liturgy of the Hours.
Appleton, George, ed. *The Oxford Book of Prayer* (New York: Oxford Univ. Press, 1985).
Boyd, Malcolm. *Are You Running With Me Jesus?* (New York: Holt, Rinehart, and Winston, 1973).
Carroll, James. *Tender of Wishes* (Paramus: Newman, 1969).
Guardini, Romano. *Prayers from Theology* (Grand Rapids: Eerdmans, 1970).
Hays, Edward. *Prayers for the Domestic Church* (Easton, Ks.: Forest Peace, 1979).
Hays, Edward. *Prayers for the Servants of God,* 1980.
Hays, Edward. *Pray All Ways,* 1981.
Hollings, Michael, and Etta Gullick. *It's Me, O Lord* (New York: Doubleday, 1973).

Nouwen, Henri. *A Cry for Mercy* (New York: Doubleday, 1983).
Sergio, Lisa, ed. *Prayers of Women* (New York: Harper and Row, 1968).
West, Herbert B. *Stay With Me, Lord: A Man's Prayers* (New York: Seabury, 1974).

2. Compare the works of a founder of a school of spirituality to a contemporary version of that spirituality, such as the revised Rule, Constitution, or reflections on the meanings of that spirituality today.

SOME SOURCES

Rule of St. Benedict (Collegeville: The Liturgical Press, 1981) might be compared to works like *Climb Along the Cutting Edge*, Joan Chittister, ed. (New York: Paulist, 1977); *The Continuing Quest for God*, William Skudlarek, ed. (Collegeville: The Liturgical Press, 1982); "St. Benedict Today," *Cistercian Studies* 3 (1979) 205-18; issues of *Benedictines;* etc.

The Spiritual Exercises of St. Ignatius, published in a variety of translations and commentaries, might be compared to present reflections on contemporary applications like *Studies in the Spirituality of the Jesuits.*

Esser, K. *Rule and Testament of St. Francis* (Chicago: Franciscan Herald Press, 1977) could be compared to interpretations of that spirituality in works like Concilium 149, *Francis of Assisi Today,* Christian Duquoc and Casiano Floristan, eds. (New York: Seabury, 1981) esp. Parts II and III.

3. Look up the origin of various festivals of Christ and Mary. Is there a discernible link between the festival and the ecclesial-cultural situation that called for such a celebration? How are Marian feasts linked to Christology? Some feasts that could be researched include: Christmas, Corpus Christi, Christ the King, Ascension, the Sacred Heart, Precious Blood, Good Friday; Immaculate Conception, Seven Sorrows, Visitation, Queenship of Mary, Assumption.

SOME SOURCES

The New Catholic Encyclopedia, vol. 17 (Washington, D.C.: Catholic
University of America, 1967) is an adequate reference.
A Dictionary of Mary, compiled by Donald Attwater (New York:
Kenedy, 1956).
The Oxford Dictionary of the Christian Church (Oxford: Oxford Uni-
versity Press, 1977).
Concilium 168, *Mary in the Churches,* Hans Küng, Jürgen Molt-
mann, eds. (New York: Seabury, 1983).
Any history of festivals could be used.

4. The liturgical year is the only source of life direction for many
in the Christian community. Reflect upon the themes developed
in the seasons of Advent, Christmas-Epiphany, Lent, Easter, and
construct thematic life direction possibilities from the texts represented in prayers, prefaces, solemn blessings, and readings.

SOME SOURCES

Sacramentary, Lectionary, and comparable books of worship.

TWO

JEWISH LITURGICAL SPIRITUALITY

You shall be holy, for I, the Lord your God, am holy
(Lv 19:2)

THE PURPOSE OF JEWISH LITURGICAL SPIRITUALITY IS TO ENABLE GOD'S
people to be holy as the Lord God is holy. For the devout Jew,
everything that is done, everything that happens can be an
epiphany of the Lord. To be holy is to be in communion with the
covenant God who is always near. The devout Jew has the wisdom to know, to see, and to bless the God who never abandons
the people. Blessing and praise of God is at the heart of Jewish life.
The prayer of blessing and praise, the berakah, makes "every action of the devout Israelite a sacred, a truly liturgical action."[1]

To understand the liturgical spirituality of Judaism, the interdependent coordinates of that spirituality, Torah and cultic liturgy, require consideration. Together, these provide a foundational structure for experiencing mythic realities of the past in a
manner that creates the holiness of the people in the present.
When Torah and cultic liturgy are understood in their interdependence, all of life can be an epiphany of the Lord. Everything
can lead to communion with the Source of life and of holiness.
Torah and cultic liturgy provide a means for becoming holy as the
Lord is holy.

1. Louis Bouyer, *The Spirituality of the New Testament and the Fathers* (New
York: Seabury, 1963) 24.

23

TORAH: SPIRITUALITY OF THE SOURCE

Torah refers to four different facets of Jewish tradition and life. It can mean the Pentateuch, the first five books of the scriptures that are kept on scrolls in an ark in the synagogue. Torah can also refer to the entire Hebrew scriptures, the Tenakh, corresponding to the Old Testament (as Christians call it). Torah can mean the disciplined, scholarly explanation and exposition of the scriptures which must be applied to changing times and conditions. Torah can also mean the meditative study of God's living Word. This reflective study enables the people to hear what God may be asking of the people, or what God may be revealing to the people at this particular time. Regardless of the meaning of Torah, every Jew is expected to study and to reflect upon God's living word. Torah is both living and a source of life because it is a source of union with the living God, whose Word creates and sustains life.[2]

> Be holy as I the Lord your God am holy (Lv 19:2).
> In the center of Torah is the Book of Leviticus.
> In the middle of Leviticus is the chapter on holiness.
> At the core of the chapter on holiness is the command
> to love your neighbor as yourself.
> In the midst of Israel is the individual Jew, trying to
> begin by loving the neighbor, and finally to become holy
> as God is holy.[3]

The life of Torah is meant to foster a perpetual awareness of the Source of life. Torah could be considered a metaphor for the mutuality of God with the people. The life of the community in dialogue with God is formed within Torah, but Torah is also an active, creative reality. Torah is an expression of the mutuality of God with the people. One way the dialogue is expressed is through the commandments, or mitzvot.

2. Jacob Neusner, *The Life of Torah: Readings in the Jewish Religious Experience* (Belmont: Dickenson Publishing Co., 1974) 25.
3. Ruth F. Brin, *Interpretation for the Weekly Torah Reading* (Minneapolis: Lerner Publications Co., 1965) 16ff.

Commandments: Source of Joy

The commandments or mitzvot are religious deeds, actions that unite the fervent Jew to the Source of holiness and joy. The 613 commandments of Torah are not perceived as a burden, but rather as a joy and a blessing. "To the nations of the earth, God gave some few laws. But his love for Israel was particularly manifested by the fullness and completeness of the Torah."[4]

This joy, a joy resulting from the performance of religious actions called commandments, was a sign of union with the Source. If someone did not know this joy, they were not acting in the spirit of the commandments. If a spirit of joy was absent, prayer should be postponed. Why? Prayer is an expression of the joyful union with God, a joyful communion that is manifest through God's holy people. Certain moods are not appropriate to prayer. This is a reason for the rabbinic teaching, "One should not commence prayer in a mood of sadness, indolence, hilarity," but rather in the spirit of joy that proceeds from union with the Source of holiness.[5]

Because the purpose of commandments was the union of the community with God, the spirit of the commandments was more important than the strict observance of all 613 prescriptions. The number of the commandments had symbolic value according to some of the rabbis. Rabbi Simlai taught the symbolic nature of the commandments by comparing the 365 prohibitive commandments to the days of the year, and the 248 affirmative commandments to the limbs of the human body. The total number, 613, was a way of demonstrating that all the actions of a person performed in time can be holy.

Simlai also showed the spirit of the commandments to be more important than the actual number by showing the summaries of commandments given by holy people. David reduced the number to eleven (Ps 15). Isaiah reduced the number to six (Is 33:25-26). Micah reduced the number to three (Mi 6:8). Second Isaiah

4. A rabbinic teaching quoted in Trepp, *The Life of Torah* 87.
5. Rabbinic teaching quoted by Norman Solomon, "God the Lawgiver—Meditations on the Spirituality of the Halakha," in *Spirituality and Prayer: Jewish and Christian Understandings*, ed. Leon Klenicki and Gabe Huck (New York: Paulist Press, 1983) 71.

reduced the number to two (56:1). Amos reduced the number to one, as did Habakkuk (Am 5:14; Hb 2:4).[6]

What is important is that it is the spirit of Torah, God's spirit, that unites the people and their God. That spirit enables Torah to be and to remain a living word of dialogue. This dialogue is between a living God and an historical people. Thus, Torah will need ongoing interpretation and creation as the life of the people continues. Ongoing interpretations of rules and relationships are necessary so that Torah can continue to address the changing circumstances of time, history, and the people of God. These ongoing interpretations and creation of Torah form the living system called the halakha.

Halakha: The Ongoing Creation of Torah

Torah, the totality of the way to holiness through union with the Source, resides in the heart of the community. For that reason the interpretation of it must be done in the midst of the community. The authentic interpreters must be one with the spirit of Torah within the community as well as one with the spirit of the Source, the living God.

One tradition of the rabbi, Hallel, brings out the emphasis on the role of the community in the formation of Torah. On one occasion of Passover, there was a question about the proper way to perform various rituals accompanying the great festival. Hillel was approached by sages to make a judgment on the matter at hand. Rather than make an educated pronouncement, which a rabbi of his status could surely have done, Hillel counseled the sages to wait before they made any decision. Instead, they were to watch what the people did, and then consider the issue again. Why consider the practices of the community? Because "if they are not prophets, they are the descendants of the prophets."[7]

Those who interpreted the Torah, the rabbis, could interpret with authenticity to the degree they touched the whole truth. The whole truth included being a lifelong student of Torah, a listener

6. Solomon Schechter, *Some Aspects of Rabbinic Theology* (New York: Schocken Books, 1961) 138-47.
7. TB Pesahim 66a, quoted by Solomon, "God the Lawgiver," in *Spirituality and Prayer*, ed. Klenicki and Huck, 75.

close to the heart of the community, and a person in touch with the heart of God. Integrity, humility, wisdom, and a great love were to be the hallmarks of those who lived the truth, and so who could interpret and simultaneously create the Torah. That person could interpret for others.

> As He clothed the naked, so do thou clothe the naked (Gn 3:21). As the Holy One—blessed be He—visited the sick (Gn.18:1), so shalt thou visit the sick ... The Torah begins with deeds of kindness ... and it ends with kindness, as it is written, "He buried Moses in the valley."[8]

The rabbi, a central interpreter of Torah, was expected to live life as a sign and reminder of God's love for the people. Joy, a sign of those who heard the word and kept it, was to be evidenced on the face of the rabbi. According to the school of Shammai, a holy rabbi was to "say little and do much, and receive every person with a cheerful face."[9] Rabbi Gamaliel urged that those "who work in behalf of the community work with them for the sake of heaven."[10]

The greatness and totality of God's living Word, Torah, allowed for opposing interpretations of that Word. It was not necessary for two rabbis to agree on the interpretation of the law. In a rabbinic tale two famous rabbis disagreed on the meaning and interpretation of a scripture passage. Each gave an interpretation that contradicted the other's interpretation. The prophet Elijah was asked to render a judgment, for Elijah was in heaven and had a better view of the whole Truth. What was Elijah's judgment? "Both are words of the living God!"[11]

How can this be possible? If two scholars disagree on the meaning of the word of God, is not one right and the other wrong? According to the sages, as long as the interpreters are humble, pious, wise, and live in the compassion of God, each interpretation is

---

8. Sota 14a, quoted by Leo Trepp, *Judaism: Development and Life* (Belmont: Dickenson, 1974) 172-73.
9. Abot 1:15, quoted by Trepp, *Judaism* 172.
10. Abot 2:2, quoted by Trepp, *Judaism* 172.
11. TB Gittin 6b, quoted by Solomon, "God the Lawgiver," in *Spirituality and Prayer*, ed. Klenicki and Huck, 74.

right. God's Word is always a greater mystery than human interpretation. The totality of Torah, the fullness of its meaning, lies
ahead and not in the past. The past should be consulted, but
neither the past nor the present can contain the fullness of the
truth of God's Word. Thus, contradictory interpretations may
both be "right." For Hillel the truth of Torah was in the fruit of action that furthered love. "What is hateful to yourself, do not do to
your fellow-man. That is the whole Torah. All the rest is commentary."[12]

Torah, the living Word, recalls and creates the dialogue of God
with the people. This people, set apart to be sacred to the Lord,
were formed through the mythic symbols of creation, exodus or
redemption, and ongoing revelation. These basic symbols provide a structure for interpreting and directing the events of
everyday. The cultic liturgy focused the meaning of these symbols. Torah was read in the midst of the liturgical community, call-
ing the community to renew the meanings of the myths of origin,
present, and future of God's people. Torah and cultic liturgy provide spiritual or life direction for the ongoing formation of the
people of God.

CULTIC LITURGY: A SPIRITUALITY THAT IS FORMATIVE OF IDENTITY

In a general sense, the life of the Jew can be considered as a life
lived in the context of liturgical spirituality. Cultic liturgy expresses and forms the devout Jew into that life. Cultic liturgy occurs at particular times. It has a particular history founded in the
past that retains meaning in the present. The richness of Jewish
cultic liturgy cannot be captured in a brief section of selected texts
and festivals. The changing liturgical expressions of Judaism that
grew out of the history of the people is a major study. Contemporary communities within the Jewish tradition exhibit a variety
of cultic similarities and differences. That too is a major study.

This section will consider selected seasonal festivals as illustrations of the formative nature of Jewish liturgical spirituality.
Daily, weekly, and seasonal cycles of liturgical celebration en-

12. Nahum Glatzer, *Hillel the Elder: The Emergence of Classical Judaism*
(Washington: Bnai Brith Hillel Foundations, 1959) 74.

hance the daily, weekly, and seasonal unfolding of life itself. The community that gathers, or the individual Jew who prays with the awareness of the community, sets aside cultic moments to be reminded of the holiness of all moments lived in the sanctuary of God, the world God created holy.

Daily Prayer: The Rhythmic Miracle of Sunrise and Sunset

The rhythmic miracle of sunrise and sunset provides a natural context for acknowledging the miracle of the lifetime of God's people. In the morning and in the evening the history and meaning of being a people sacred to the Lord is recalled with thanks. The new day provides the setting for experiencing creation, redemption, and covenant once again.

> Blessed is the Eternal, our God, who has awakened me to the new day ... Help me Lord, to be awake to this day, to the wonders that surround me, alive to beauty and love, aware that all being is precious, and that we walk on holy ground wherever we go.[13]

Each morning and evening the credo of Jewish faith is recited. This credo, called the Shema, is part of every liturgy. "Hear, O Israel: the Lord is our God. The Lord is One. Blessed be his glorious kingdom forever and ever!" (Dt 6:4)

A rich variety of blessings, berakah, praise God for the ongoing intimacy of the covenant that continues to be formative of the people. The blessings can vary with the particular season of the year, but always God is praised for the revelation that continues everyday.

> Deep is your love for us, O Lord, our God. Bounteous is your compassion and tenderness ... Endow us with discernment and understanding. Enlighten our eyes in your Torah ... Open our hearts to your commandments ... You have drawn us close to you. We praise you who chose your people in love.[14]

13. *Gates of the House: The New Union Home Prayer Book* (New York: Central Conference of American Rabbis, 1977) 2, 3.
14. Second Blessing, *Weekday Prayer Book* (New York: Rabbinical Assembly, 1962) 45-46.

The people chosen in love remember what it means to be that people sacred to the Lord. "You shall love the Lord your God with all your heart, with all your soul, and with all your strength. Take to heart these words which I enjoin on you today." (Dt 6:4-9). "If then you truly heed my commandments which I enjoin on you today, loving and serving the Lord your God with all your heart and all your soul, I will . . . " (Dt 11:13-21) A third reading recalls the meaning of the tassels on the corners of garments. "You will remember to keep all my commandments and be holy to your God. I, the Lord, am your God who, as God, brought you out of the land of Egypt, that I the Lord, may be your God." (Nm 15:37-41)

The three readings present the living memory of what it means to be and to become a people set apart for the Lord. But even humans who actively remember the call to be holy as the Lord is holy, remain caught in a tension. Who one may wish to be is not always acted out. The tension between who one is and who one might like to be is resolved in the mystery of God's redemption of the people. Every day, recreation and redemption express the nature of the living covenant.

> You have ever been our redeemer and deliverer. There can be no God but you . . . Our redeemer is the Holy One of Israel, the Lord of hosts is his name. Praised are you, O Lord, Redeemer of Israel.[15]

Each day the Jew remembers that the Lord God continues to create, to reveal, and to redeem the people. Each day, though the morning and evening prayer may be said privately, there is a solidarity with the community sacred to the Lord. It is the community of Israel who proclaim their belief that "The Lord is One." (Dt 4) Each day the community remembers that all ground can be holy ground, for the presence of the Lord is manifest through all times and places. In the evening, those who have walked in the presence of the Lord can fall peacefully asleep.

> Lord, Guardian of Israel, you neither slumber nor sleep. Blessed are you by day, and blessed by night; blessed when we lie down,

15. *Weekday Prayer Book* 50ff.

blessed when we rise up . . . Let your good presence hover at my side . . . Grant that I may lie down in peace and rise up to life renewed. Hear O Israel: the Lord is our God, the Lord is One.[16]

Daily prayer provides an integral environment of mythic symbols to give meaning to events. Creation, redemption, and revelation are continuous events in the history of intimacy of God with the people. But meaningful daily living requires periods of more restful renewal than the daily experience of patterned work and life allow. This weekly day of renewal is called the Sabbath.

The Sabbath: The Lord's Day

The Sabbath, Shabbat, is a weekly recreation. The Sabbath has typically been called "a day of rest," but the "rest" has a sacred meaning. When the Sabbath is kept, the Servant of God, Israel, remembers that the work of servants has meaning only insofar as that work is really the work of the Master. Keeping the Sabbath is doing the Master's work. Refusing to keep the Sabbath by doing work of human choosing is not the work of the Master. That is the work of foolish and unprofitable servants.

Doing the work of the Master requires that time be set aside to be renewed, to rest awhile in the peace of the Lord. Otherwise, the work of human hands may cease to create the world into the sanctuary of the Lord. So the Sabbath is celebrated as a special day of remembrance of the creative and compassionate acts of God to the Jewish people and to all people.

The Sabbath ritual is a family ritual that begins on the eve of the Sabbath with a festively set table. Before beginning this celebration, it is customary for the members of the family to contribute something to the poor. Thus, the compassion of God is lived in a small way before the formal remembrance and renewal begins. As dusk settles, the family joins around the festively set table.

As we begin this day of holiness, we shall not forget the words of your prophet who called us to share our bread with the hungry, to clothe the naked, and never to hide ourselves from our own kin.[17]

16. *Gates of the House* 4-5.
17. *Gates of the House* 29.

Candles are kindled, and the meaning of this symbol is ritually focused. "As this brightness reminds us of the generations of Israel who have kindled light, so may we in our own day, be among those who kindle light."[18] A variety of blessings, berakah, may follow. A wife or mother, a husband or father, could be remembered as a blessing to those around the table.

> A woman of valor, seek her out, for she is to be valued above rubies. Her husband trusts her ... She opens her hand to those in need and offers her help to the poor ... Her life proclaims her praise (Prv 31).

> Blessed is the man who reveres the Lord, who greatly delights in God's commandments ... Light dawns in the Darkness for the upright, for the one who is gracious, compassionate, and just ... His heart is steady ... he has given to the poor (Ps 112).[19]

Blessings over the wine and bread recall the joy of being God's people, a people constantly recreated in God's love. "We rejoice that we are created in the divine image."[20] Blessing and thanks are also given for the home, a living symbol of the sacred sanctuary the world is intended to be.

> We give thanks, O God, for family and home. May it be warm with love and companionship. Here may we always find rest from the day's work, and refuge from cares. May our joys be deepened, and our griefs softened by the love we give and receive.[21]

Children receive a blessing from the parents. The blessing is simultaneously an instruction, an invitation, and an invocation. It reminds children that they are the living memory of the tradition of God's people, and it is they who must keep the memory alive.

> May God bless you and guide you. Be strong for the truth, charitable in your words, just and loving in your deeds. A noble heritage

18. *Gates of the House* 30.
19. *Gates of the House* 33.
20. Kiddush for the Eve of Shabbat, *Gates of the House* 33.
21. *Gates of the House* 31.

has been entrusted to you . . . The Lord bless and keep you; the Lord look kindly upon you and be gracious to you; the Lord bestow his favor upon you and give you peace.[22]

A moment of silence provides time for each to remember the others at the table with silent blessing. The eve of the Sabbath is concluded. The evening belongs to God alone.

In the morning, public worship will be attended. The Torah will be read and explained. The family, upon returning home, will meet again around the table to hear a special blessing, the kiddush. "It is a sign forever between me and the people of Israel . . . The Lord blessed the seventh day and called it holy."[23] A joyful meal follows. The rest of the day is a time for recreation. The eve of the Sabbath belonged to God alone. The day of the Sabbath is for the creative leisure and joy of God's people. This leisure includes reflection upon the Torah.

Sabbath concludes with the evening service of farewell. As the stars rise in the skies, the people gather publicly. The sacred day, set apart from other days to serve as reminder of the people set apart for the Lord, is a source of blessing for which the night prayer gives thanks. A cup, filled to overflowing, is raised. The people ask God for blessings overflowing into the week ahead. A tower shaped vessel filled with sweet smelling spices is passed to the people as a symbol of the sweetness of the Sabbath. Inhaling this sweetness, the people ask that the delight of God accompany them through the week until the next Sabbath.

Peace and a good week are wished to all. The renewal experienced on this day continues to serve as a rhythmic reminder that life requires time for renewal and remembering. If the Lord does not build the house, they labor in vain who try to do it. Union with the Source of life is remembered on the Sabbath.

Night descends and great is our song which breaks through to the heavens . . . Our path has no end, for our heart is one heart, now and always.[24]

22. *Gates of the House* 32.
23. *Gates of the House* 35.
24. Song for Shabbat, Rad Halaila, *Gates of the House* 40.

The rhythm of remembering creation, redemption, and liberation extends to the seasons as well as the weekly cycle. The meaning of the events of the past for interpreting the present and the future is ritually focused in the seasonal festivals. Some seasonal festivals will be singled out to illustrate how the liturgy of festivals contributes to the spiritual formation of the people.

The Days of Awe: The New Year, Rosh Hashanah to Yom Kippur

The Days of Awe are fall festivals which usher in the New Year. The New Year begins with an eight-day period, extending from Rosh Hashanah to Yom Kippur. The solemn entrance into the New Year is marked by reconciliation with God and with each other. How can there be a better world built on peace and love if the covenant people cannot live in peace and love?

Rosh Hashanah begins with each member of the family contributing something to a worthy cause. As dusk settles, the family gathers to begin the high holy days, in union with all other Jews. The communal nature of the celebration is clear.

> May we, together with the whole House of Israel, be mindful of the needs of others . . . Then shall your light blaze forth like the dawn and your wounds quickly heal.
>
> The flames we kindle are a symbol of your eternal flame: may they open our eyes to the good we must do, moving us to work for harmony and peace, and so making the world bright with your presence . . .
>
> May our worship on this day fill us with eagerness to embrace life and to hallow it. May the New Year bring renewed strength to our people Israel, and peace to the world.[25]

Various blessings are remembered by the people. In particular, the blessing of being God's people is remembered with thanks. Following Rosh Hashanah, the seven days of awe will be days to return to the Lord, to be renewed in holiness, and so to live in a new way as God's people. Yom Kippur, the holiest day of the year,

---

25. *Gates of the House* 49, 51.

is a Day of Atonement. As the lights are kindled on the eve of Yom Kippur, an opening prayer states the purpose of this time.

> The holiest day of the year is about to begin. Let us use it well. May it be for each of us a day of renewal. May it help us to overcome what is evil in us, and to strengthen what is good. May it bring us closer to one another, and make us more loyal to our community, our faith and our God.[26]

Before celebrating the day of Yom Kippur, each person must seek out any enemy and ask forgiveness. The offended party must graciously forgive the one asking for forgiveness. This is the way the forgiveness of God shall be known. For the twenty-four hours of Yom Kippur, no food or drink may be taken. No symbol of earthly care or concern must enter the mind and heart of the Jew who stands before God.

All prayers during this period of time include some confession of sin. This confession is recited privately for God alone to hear. But there is a community recitation as well to acknowledge the mutual responsibility that each person has for all other people. "Is not this the fast I have chosen? To loose the fetters of wickedness, to undo the bonds of the yoke, to let the oppressed go free." (Is 58:5-7)

Yom Kippur is the only festival of the year during which the Jew kneels. If kneeling were to be done at any other time, it could be misunderstood as the burden of life pressing the person down. On the day of Yom Kippur, it cannot be misinterpreted. For on this day the people kneel as symbol of all humanity bending the knee before the Lord of all time and place. Kneeling is a symbol of trust that the future of God shall come, and this people will work toward the coming of that future.

The Book of Jonah is read on this day. This book is recited to make it clear that God's love and forgiveness are not reserved for the Jews only. "Shall I not have pity on Nineveh, that great city, in which there are more than 120,000 people who cannot tell their right hand from their left?" (Jon 4:11)[27]

As a link in a chain, the closing prayer brings together the past

26. *Gates of the House* 56.
27. Trepp, *Judaism* 234-36.

and the future. The closing prayer recalls those who have died. As the stars rise in the sky, the congregation affirms the vision of the kingdom of God that lies ahead. It affirms as well its willingness to bring about that kingdom in the year ahead. "Hear, O Israel. The Lord our God, the Lord is One." (Dt 6:4)

The Festival of Tabernacles: Nothing But Joy

The days of awe are a preparation for days of thanksgiving and joy. Tabernacles or Sukkot are festival days of thanks that are observed for seven days. The festival is named after the booths or tents which the people dwelt in when God led them from Egypt (Lv 23:42). The Tabernacle or booth is a symbol of the love and peace experienced by the people on the journey toward a promised land. In spite of periods of homelessness, God was a shelter to the people. God's care is symbolized by the tent. In the love of this God, all humankind can dwell secure.

The life of the people of God is one marked by blessings. This includes the harvest, a symbol appropriate for the fall festival. The theme of the harvest is that of thanksgiving for all the blessings of God to the people.

> Eternal Lord, God of our people, let your presence dwell among us. Spread over us the tabernacle of your peace. Be with us on this Festival, as with love and awe we celebrate Your greatness and Your infinite goodness to all the living. We build this Sukkah with joy and gratitude for the gift of life and for all that sustains our bodies and enriches our spirits. Blessed be the Lord our God . . . for giving us life, for sustaining us, and for enabling us to reach this season.[28]

After building the booth or tent, the people are urged to invite guests, especially the poor. This is a gesture of gratitude to God who has been constantly gracious to the people. Members of the community of the past are ritually summoned to symbolize the unity of the community.

> Lord our God and God of our mothers and fathers, be present among us, spread over us the shelter of Your peace and surround

---

28. *Gates of the House* 76.

us with your radiance . . . Let there be food and drink for all who hunger and thirst. Blessed be the Lord forever . . . To this meal, we summon sublime guests: Abraham, Isaac, Jacob . . . Sarah, Rebekah, Rachel, Leah . . . Holy be my thoughts, in token of the abundance of blessing that is mine from heaven and earth.[29]

The thanksgiving festival of joy ends and the days of winter approach. In the midst of the season of shortened days and longer nights, the feast of light occurs.

Hanukkah: The Feast of Light

The feast of light is historically rooted in the restoration and rededication of the temple during the time of the Maccabees (1 Macc 4:36-61; 2 Macc). Hanukkah, like the two subsequent festivals, is a minor holiday. Major holidays are those ordained by God in the Pentateuch. Minor festivals are "human institutions created at various times in history and fashioned by the Rabbis into religious occasions."[30]

As the lights of Hanukkah are kindled, a prayer indicates the variety of meanings the festival has accumulated. Like other festivals, the core historical meaning becomes a foundation for the interpretation of the present and future.

Within living memory, our people was plunged into deepest darkness. But we endured; the light of faith still burns brightly . . . Let the lights we kindle shine forth for the world . . . The people who walked in darkness have seen a great light . . . Torah is light. Arise, shine, for your light has come . . . The Lord shall be your everlasting light.[31]

Other minor festivals occur on the path toward spring. The primary festival of spring is passover, celebrated on 15th Nisan. Because of the importance of this festival for Jewish identity, this festival has a preparatory day, the 10th Nisan. The joy of the prep-

29. *Gates of the House* 78.
30. Leo Trepp, *The Complete Book of Jewish Observance* (New York: Behrman House, Inc., 1980) 136.
31. *Gates of the House* 80, 82.

aration is an anticipation of this joyous feast of being a people sacred to the Lord.

Passover: The Night Different from Other Nights

Passover or Pessah is the feast of eternal revelation and everlasting challenge for the Jewish people. Passover means life, liberty, the pursuit of justice, and inalienable rights given by God to all people. The centrality of the Passover festival in the spirituality of the Jews can be witnessed to by the remembrance of it in daily, weekly, and seasonal prayer. The lessons to be learned from the Exodus are many.

It was the Lord "who brought you out of the land of Egypt, the house of bondage." (Ex 20:2) Because Israel knew what it was like to be a stranger, God says, "the stranger . . . thou shalt love as thyself." (Lv 19:34) Passover was a night different from all other nights, for on this night Israel came to know the Lord God in an intimate way. As that night is remembered, the history of God's people, past, present, and to come, is highly ritualized in the Passover Supper.

The basic setting and ritual of Passover can be found in Ex 12-13, Lv 23, and Dt 16. The order of the supper, Seder, provides a dramatic ritual that makes use of many symbols. These symbols summarize the past, present, and future of the people of God. A festive table is set. The passover story and its meaning, haggadah, will be set at each place. Each place will also have a wine cup. This cup will be filled at four points in the ritual, symbolizing the four cups of freedom (Ex 6:6-7). An extra cup, the fifth cup of Elijah, will be set by the leader's place. This cup, the promise of redemption for all people, is linked to Elijah, the messenger of the fulfillment of the kingdom of God (Mal 3:22-24). Elijah's cup will not be drunk, for it is to serve as a reminder of the way the people must live to hasten the coming of the kingdom of God.

Three portions of unleavened bread, matzot, are placed by the leader, representing the priests, levites, and other people redeemed equally by the Lord. A roasted shankbone reminds the family of the paschal lamb, once offered in the temple. The pitcher for washing hands is placed by the leader's side. Other symbolic foods include an egg, bitter herbs, a green vegetable, and a mixture called haroseth. These foods are symbols of new life, suffering endured in the past, the mortar made by the enslaved people, and the transformation of all of this by God.

The service begins with a blessing of children by the parents. The mother kindles the candles. Then the leader blesses the day and the first cup of wine, mixing water and spices into the wine. All drink the first cup. The leader, after washing hands, distributes parsley or lettuce, and a portion of matzah. "This is the bread of poverty our people ate in the land of Egypt . . . May those who are cast out in the streets come and join our celebration."[32]

The leader mixes a second cup of wine and the youngest child asks, "Why is this night different from other nights?" The leader responds with the passover story and its meanings, the haggadah. As the story describes the ten plagues, a finger is dipped into the wine and a drop of wine flicked out of the cup. This symbolizes that the suffering of anyone, even enemies, diminishes the joy of the people of God. "Rejoice not when your enemies are afflicted," says Proverbs (24:17). The shankbone, matzah, and bitter herbs are raised as an explanation of their meaning is given. Then the second cup of wine is raised. All join together saying, "Therefore we must thank God in every way for all the miracles. Let us recite the Hallel." The first part of the Hallel, Psalms 113 and 114, precedes the drinking of the second cup of thanksgiving.

The leader and everyone at the table wash their hands. The two unbroken matzah are blessed with the berakah for bread. Breaking the matzah, the leader gives a piece to each person. Blessings are repeated, and the matzah is eaten. Bitter herbs are blessed, passed, and eaten. In memory of Hillel, the respected teacher, a matzah and horseradish sandwich is consumed. This recalls the challenging summary that Hillel gave of Torah. The fulfillment of Torah is in loving God through loving one's neighbor.

Finally, the meal is served. As the meal nears completion, the children may search for the matzah that had been hidden earlier. When the meal ends, the hidden matzah is consumed without any blessing. No more food may be eaten after this. Grace follows, a hymn is sung, and a third cup of thanksgiving for the bounties of the present is drunk.

Finally, the ritual looks to the future. A door is opened for Eli-

32. Trepp, *Judaism* 245-49.

jah, as all sing, "May he come to us with the Messiah."[33] Before the door is closed, various scriptural passages are recited or sung (Ps 79:6-7; Ps 69:25; Lam 3:66). The remainder of the Hallel is recited (Ps 115-118), then the great Hallel is recited (Ps 136). A Sabbath hymn precedes the raising and drinking of the fourth cup of wine, a toast to the future. The Song of Songs or other fitting passages or hymns may conclude the ritual. The rest of the night is for enjoying the memory. No one will leave the house.

The intimate love of God and the people are renewed on this night. Passover recalls and renews the identity of God's people as a people sacred to the Lord. The spring setting of the feast provides a seasonal environment conducive to the recreation and future hope motifs celebrated in the feast. Passover celebration continues for seven days, with men and women alternating in leading the services.[34] As Passover concludes, the march toward another festival begins. Seven weeks after Passover, the Feast of Weeks, Shavuot, occurs.

Shavuot: Receiving the Living Word

Shavuot commemorates the giving of the Torah to the people. This important festival has few symbols compared to other major festivals. Though synagogues will be well decorated on this day, there is a conscious awareness that the day should have few symbols. Nothing can really symbolize the great gift and mystery of God's living Word given to the people.

A Hasidic tradition points to the reason why the festival is called the giving of Torah rather than the receiving of Torah. "The giving was on Shavuot; the receiving must take place every day."[35]

During the celebration of Shavuot the Book of Ruth will be read. This book is read to remind the people that the Torah is meant for all people, not only for the Jews. In a way, that Torah is lived by anyone who lives with a compassion like God's, who acts responsibly for others, and who is an agent of redemption or liberation for the people who are met in life. If God's Word is a liv-

33. Trepp, *Jewish Observance* 189.
34. Trepp, *Judaism* 245-49.
35. Kotzer Rebbe, quoted in Trepp, *Jewish Observance* 203.

ing Word, in the heart before it is on the lips, the potential universality of God's revelation must be acknowledged.

Reform Judaism initiated the custom of having young women
and men confirm their allegiance to Torah on Shavuot, as their an-
cestors once did at Sinai. In the nineteenth century, this temporarily replaced the Bar and Bat Mitzvah in Reformed Judaism.
Today the Bar and Bat Mitzvah are again celebrated. However, the
practice of confirmation of faith on Shavuot remains a focal symbol of the meaning of this day. "The giving was on Shavuot; the
receiving must take place every day."[36]

SUMMARY

To become holy as the Lord God is holy is the hope of the people set apart to be sacred to the Lord. All of life is meant to be an
epiphany of the Lord's presence with and for the people. In its
general meaning, liturgical spirituality provides the context for
the meaning of Jewish identity. The Torah, the living Word of the
Lord, is spoken to the heart of the community. Cultic liturgy provides the setting for remembering and renewing that union with
the Lord.

Torah, the living Word of the Lord, is received every day by the
devout Jew. "It is something very near to you, already in your
mouths and in your heart . . . You have only to carry it out." (Dt
30:11, 13) Torah is continually formed through the dialogue of
God with the heart of the community. Thus the living Word never
ceases to be spoken. It is heard anew by every generation. This
presupposes that its interpretation will continue to be applied in
ways appropriate to ever-changing times, conditions, and people.

Those who interpret and apply the living Word to specific
situations must be living symbols of the compassion of God. They
must also be serious lifelong students of the Word of God.
Though every Jew is expected to be serious about knowing the
Word that is lived in everyday life, the rabbi is expected to have
more profound wisdom. Always, the listening of the rabbi occurs
in the midst of the community which hears. Listening to the heart
of God requires listening to the heart of the community.

Torah, with its commandments and other blessings, is for all of

36. Trepp, *Jewish Observance* 203.

life. The Jew who lives in the spirit of Torah finds all of life a
source of liturgy, for the Lord can be praised and blessed at all
times. Cultic liturgy sets aside time in daily, weekly, and seasonal
rhythms to renew the people in the great mysteries of creation,
redemption, and ongoing liberation.

Seasonal festivals accent the mystery of God's love for the people throughout the history of the people. Such accents are
necessary for renewing and being re-created into the living
memory of the people. Life can become routine when such accents are not acknowledged. The transition through the seasons
reminds the people that their God journeys with them at all
seasons of their communal and personal history.

Symbols of the past continue to provide foundational myths for
interpreting the present and the future. The great pilgrimage festivals of Sukkot, Passover, and Pentecost are special moments on
the journey. But all the festivals point to the intimacy of God's ongoing presence to the people. The universality of God's revelation
and compassion becomes the horizon for the compassion of the
people. Even the suffering of enemies reduces the joy of God's
people, as Passover points out.

Cultic liturgy is a major source of spiritual formation, for it provides communal moments that are meant to give meaning to the
mystery of being God's people. Whether it is daily prayer, weekly
observance, or seasonal celebrations, each recalls that it is the
community that has been set apart for the Lord. To be holy as God
is holy means to be formed by, but also formative of, the community. The community, in union with the compassion of God for
all people, must extend beyond itself. The prayers of the liturgical
feasts clearly extend care beyond the assembled community to the
world.

"You shall be holy," says God, "for I, the Lord your God, am
holy." (Lv 19:2) The challenge of Torah, the living Word, is a
power that can transform individual holiness into communal holiness, and communal holiness into deeper individual holiness.
Jewish liturgical spirituality, focused through Torah and cultic
liturgy, provided a formative identity for Jesus Christ, the rabbi
from Nazareth.

As a rabbi, Jesus Christ would interpret Torah and provide an
ongoing creation of it as well. Like other rabbis, he would summarize and synthesize the spirit of Torah into blessings, and even

into one law, "Love one another as I have loved you." Like other rabbis, he would attract some disciples and he would create some enemies. Jesus Christ claimed that he had "not come to abolish the law and the prophets, but to fulfill them." (Mt 5:17) What interpretations of Torah led to his suffering and death? Halakha was a legitimate function of the rabbis whose lives of disciplined study and compassion put them in meaningful union with the Source of Torah, Jahweh.

Why then were there relatively few followers who believed in the teachings, miracles, and life, death, resurrection of the rabbi from Nazareth? Was his proclamation of the kingdom of God different than the people hoped for? Were his claims too radical and his discipleship too radical to appeal to the majority? The next chapter will address these issues in context of the age in which Jesus Christ lived, and the abiding memory he left with those who believed.

FURTHER THEMATIC DEVELOPMENT

1. Compare specific rituals of Judaism, including the symbols and prayer texts, to similar liturgical rituals in Christianity, for example, circumcision with infant baptism; Bat and Bar Mitzvah with confirmation; marriage; death or mourning rituals.

SOME SOURCES

The Book of Common Prayer.
The Book of Worship for Church and Home.
Gates of the House: The New Union Home Prayer Book.
Gates of Mitzvah.
Gates of Repentance.
The Lutheran Book of Worship.
The Rites, 2 vols. (New York: Pueblo, 1983, 1979).
Hertz, Rabbi Joseph, ed. *The Jewish Prayer Book: Siddur* (New York: Bloch, 1965).
Klein, Isaac. *A Guide to Jewish Religious Practice* (New York: Jewish Theological Seminary of America, 1979).
Trepp, Leo. *The Complete Book of Jewish Observance* (New York: Behrman House, Inc., 1980).

Trepp, Leo. *Judaism, Development and Life* (Belmont: Dickenson, 1974).

2. Morning and evening prayers use symbols of nature to reflect on human life in relationship to God. Compare the thematic and symbolic similarities and differences between the morning and evening prayers of Jewish and Christian tradition.

SOME SOURCES

The Book of Common Prayer.
Gates of the House: The New Union Home Prayer Book.
The Jewish Prayer Book: Siddur.
The Liturgy of the Hours (New York: Catholic Book Publishing Company, 1975).
The Lutheran Book of Worship.
Huck, Gabe. "Daily Prayer in Christian Tradition and Life," *Spirituality and Prayer* (New York: Paulist, 1983) 45-65.
Klein, Isaac. *A Guide to Jewish Religious Practice* (New York: Jewish Theological Seminary of America, 1979).
Trepp, Leo. *The Complete Book of Jewish Observance* (New York: Behrman House, Inc., 1980) esp. 13-26.

3. The wisdom and holiness of the rabbi in Judaism is reflected through many rabbinic tales. Compare that wisdom to the expectations of deacon, priest, and bishop in Roman Catholic ritual and tradition.

SOME SOURCES

The Rites, vol. 2.
Mintz, Jerome. *Legends of the Hasidim* (Chicago: University of Chicago Press, 1968).
Mitchell, Nathan. *Mission and Ministry* (Wilmington: Michael Glazer, 1982).
Neusner, Jacob. *The Life of Torah* 61-92.
Newman, Louis. *The Hasidic Anthology: Tales and Teachings of the Hasidim* (New York: Schocken Books, 1965).
Provost, James H., ed. *Official Ministry in a New Age* (Washington, D.C.: Catholic University of America, 1981).

Schillebeeckx, Edward. *Ministry* (New York: Crossroad, 1981).

Trepp, Leo. *Judaism: Development and Life* (Belmont: Dickenson, 1974) esp. 218-234.

Vatican II documents—

Decree on the Ministry and Life of Priests

Decree on the Pastoral Office of Bishops in the Church.

4. Compare the halakha tradition of Judaism to the ongoing revelation theme of Christian tradition. What role does the community play in creation of, and interpretation of, the halakha or Christian revelation?

SOME SOURCES

Congar, Yves. *Tradition and Traditions* (New York: Macmillan, 1967).

Mackey, James Patrick. *The Modern Theology of Tradition* (New York: Herder, 1963).

Neusner, Jacob. *The Way of Torah* (Belmont: Wadsworth, 1979) esp. 66-80, 91-95, 104-15, 124-32.

Rahner, Karl. *The Shape of the Church to Come* (New York: Seabury, 1972).

Solomon, Norman. "God the Lawgiver—Meditations on the Spirituality of the Halakha," *Spirituality and Prayer* 66-81.

Trepp, Leo. *Judaism: Development and Life* (Belmont: Dickenson, 1974) 118-29.

Trepp, Leo. *The Complete Book of Jewish Observances* (New York: Behrman House, Inc., 1980) 255-76.

Vatican II documents—

The Decree on the Apostolate of the Laity.

The Constitution on Divine Revelation.

The Constitution on the Church.

The Constitution on the Church in the Modern World.

THREE

HOLINESS AND HOPEFULNESS IN THE COMMON ERA

What must I do to enter the kingdom of God?
(Mt 19:16)

WHAT MUST I DO TO ENTER THE KINGDOM OF GOD? THE QUESTION WAS frequently asked by God's people whenever an age of renewal was upon them. For a fervent Jew the answer was always old, and yet always new. To enter the kingdom, one had only to live Torah. Torah, what was and what was yet to be, was the totality of the way to holiness. The living Word of the Lord was an ongoing dialogue of a covenant God with a covenant people. Cultic liturgy informed, formed, and expressed the heart of this people sacred to the Lord. In accented rhythms of the daily, weekly, and seasonal liturgy, the kingdom of God was actively awaited. Those who were alive to the epiphanies of God through the ordinary would glimpse the mystery of the extraordinary.

> Help me, O Lord, to be awake to this day, to the wonders that surround me, alive to beauty and love, aware that all being is precious, and that we walk on holy ground wherever we go.[1]

What must be done to enter the kingdom of God? Watching and waiting with an open heart was a key to the kingdom. Being faithful to Torah provided the vision for the kingdom. Daily

---

1. *Gates of the House* 2-3.

petitioning for the wisdom that would enable one to enter the kingdom was a constant reminder of the way to it. "Enlighten our eyes in your Torah . . . Open our hearts to your commandments."[2] Fidelity to Torah was a key to the kingdom of God.

> Whoever breaks the least significant of these commands and teaches others to do the same shall be called least in the kingdom of God.Whoever fulfills and teaches these commands shall be called great in the kingdom of God. (Mt 5:19)

Devout Jews of the common era, c.e., were experiencing a renewed kingdom fervor. A faithful remnant had lived through the infidelity and renewed fidelity to Torah, the profanation and then rededication of the temple, the bondage, dispersion, and return of the people to their homeland. Renewed fervor for the kingdom of God had accelerated once Roman rule overtook Palestine in 63 b.c.e. Varieties of religious movements gained a ready audience. Each answered the kingdom question in a slightly different manner. Each claimed to be true to Torah.

For those who accepted the halakha tradition, the ongoing application, interpretation, and creation of Torah was orthodox. People within the halakha tradition could "bring forth from the storeroom both the new and the old." (Mt 13:52) But some believers did not accept the ongoing creation of Torah. Thus the "old" was not a basic difficulty, but the ongoing evolution of old into the new. There was a felt tension over what constituted the new heart that had been prophetically promised.

> Behold the days are coming, says the Lord, when I will make a new covenant with the house of Israel . . . I will put my law within them and I will write it upon their hearts; I will be their God and they shall be my people . . . And no longer shall each teach the other . . . for they shall all know me, from the least to the greatest, says the Lord. (Jer 31:31-34)

At the time of Jesus Christ the reign of God was felt to be at hand. Israel, the people holy to its Lord, was invited to be uprooted from a predictable God and a predictable kingdom. The

2. *Weekday Prayer Book* 45-46.

kingdom movements of John the Baptist, the Pharisees, the Sadducees, the Essenes, the Zealots, and Jesus Christ announced the
nearness of the reign of God. Communities of people gathered
around particular rabbis, or teachers. In the rabbinic tradition the
proclamation of the teachers included their lives as well as their
words. Each person or movement emphasized a particular approach to Torah and to the kingdom of God. There were similarities about the conditions for entering the kingdom, but there
were also differences. There were similarities and differences in
the symbolic interpretation of temple and synagogue, gathering
places where the people experienced being a people sacred to
the Lord.

At the time of Jesus Christ the temple and the synagogue were
both popular gathering symbols for the Jewish people. A history
of evolving meanings made the temple attractive to some people
and to some kingdom movements, but repulsive to others.
Similarly, the synagogue was a symbol of religious fervor that attracted some and repelled others.

Israel, the people of God, had a sacred and subversive history.
The divine holiness that the reign of God demanded of the people
was a dangerous holiness. For some Jews the temple was central
to the cultic holiness of the community. For others the temple was
a symbol of the corruption that comes when the priests spend too
much time collecting taxes and money. Each kingdom movement
of the period proclaimed the nearness of the reign of God, including either acceptance or rejection of the temple. All movements
agreed that the kingdom would come in a manner appropriate to
the dynamism of the all-holy God, and those with faith would
know the coming.

> Biblical faith, therefore, could never be a religion of the status quo
> for its faithful adherents. Dynamic change and revolution are to be
> expected because God is a dynamic being . . . engaged in the active
> direction of history to his own goals.[3]

The kingdom question revolved around another question. Who
was most faithful to Torah, the living Word? Could it be the

3. G. E. Wright, *The Old Testament Against Its Environment* (Chicago:
Regnery, 1954) 22.

believers who clung tightly to past laws, traditions, religious expressions, and structures? Or were those more faithful to Torah whose formation from the past enabled them to accept the divine discontinuity manifest in Jesus Christ? In time, Jesus Christ would be the two-edged sword that separated the new and old brought from the storeroom.

For people in the common era Jesus Christ was at the heart of one of many movements answering kingdom questions. "What must one do to enter the kingdom of God?" "How will the kingdom come, on earth or in heaven?" "What are the signs of the coming?" The answers given by the different movements all centered around the need for the community of Israel to be converted anew.

This chapter will consider the various kingdom movements in the first century c.e. and the centrality of the temple or synagogue in those various movements. Why some movements favored the temple or the synagogue symbol of renewal may be better understood after a brief exposé of the history of each.

TEMPLE AND SYNAGOGUE: PRIESTLY AND LAY TRADITIONS

The temple tradition of the Israelites had a much longer history than that of the synagogue. Solomon centralized sacrificial worship in Jerusalem and established an official line of temple priests. However, after the exile and diaspora, 537 b.c.e., the synagogue arose as a center for a community to worship and pray, to reflect on the word of the Lord together, and to exchange ideas. Each tradition had a history of meanings that attracted different groups at the time of Jesus Christ.

Priestly Tradition of the Temple

In early Jewish history there was not a separate or official priesthood. It is not known when or how professional priests appeared in Jewish history, but it is known that the levites were specialists in priestly functions by the time the tribes settled in Palestine. Being a priest at this time meant caring for home or local sanctuaries. It also included being an oracular consultant for the head of a household or for a group of people. Such a consultation meant casting lots (sticks, stones, dice, and the like) to discover what God wished, or what the questioner was to do.

Not all levites were priests, nor were all priests at this time from the tribe of Levi. Levites became priests simply by practicing priestly functions. Since the tribe of Levi had no land base for security, priesthood was a practical occupation. It was one way to make a living (See Gn 49:3-27; Jdgs 17,18).[4]

Before the period of the monarchy prestige among the priests was determined by the household or sanctuary each serviced. If the Ark of the Covenant rested at the sanctuary, that sanctuary was prestigious. The sanctuary of Shiloh was such a sanctuary in Jewish history. It was a center of both religious and political importance. By the time of Samuel a single family of priests guarded this sanctuary. Priests were still oracular consultants, but also teachers of Torah. Individual Israelites who offered sacrifices at the sanctuary set aside some of their sacrifices for the priests. Some priests, and entire families of priests, were corrupt but they still functioned as oracles (1 Sam 1; 2).

During the time of Samuel some prophets appear who absorb the priestly role of interpreting God's will. God's will was still determined by lot, and either priest or prophet could cast lots. Samuel, and later Nathan, reflect this change in roles during the Davidic period (1 Sam 10, 13; 2 Sam 11, 12).

Two levitical lines of priests, Eli and Zadok, vied for the positions of royal priesthood under David and Solomon. Eli's line served the Davidic monarchy, while Zadok's line served the monarchy of Solomon (1 Sam 22:20-23; 1 Kgs 1:7, 8). Through both monarchies the king had ultimate authority in matters of liturgy and priesthood. The king presided at sacrificial worship and blessed the people. David and Solomon, in centralizing the worship of the people, also set forth a model of priesthood that emerged as primarily cultic. In time, more and more cultic functions were reserved to the priests, while prophets functioned as interpreters of God's will.[5]

Though David and Solomon did centralize sacrificial worship in Jerusalem, countryside shrines remained places for sacrifice.

4. Aelred Cody, *A History of Old Testament Priesthood* (Rome: Pontifical Biblical Institute, 1969), *Analecta Biblica* 35, 25-37.
5. Cody, *A History* 90-112.

The Zadokite line of levites remained attached to the worship of Jerusalem, while other priests became country priests serving less prestigious sanctuaries. Their income, as well as their prestige, was generally less than that of the temple priests.

By 609 b.c.e. Jerusalem was considered the legitimate sanctuary of Jahweh, and the priests who served here had a prestige that caused tensions. Country priests, whose work was considered far less important and far less lucrative, were looked down upon. The tensions that arose at this time remained strong. Different families of priests vied for the temple priesthood, for it became more prestigious. The Zadokites claimed to be the faithful remnant of levitical priesthood. They remained as temple priests until the second century b.c.e. (Ezek 44).

When Antiochus IV Epiphanes (175-163 b.c.e.) attempted to hellenize life in Jerusalem, there was an opposition to the Zadokite priesthood of the temple. The Maccabees led a revolt (1 Mac 1-6). The aftermath of the revolt spelled the end of the Zadokite priesthood in the temple of Jerusalem, for the Zadokites did not agree with the religious philosophy of the Maccabees.

The Maccabean ideology believed that the high priesthood of the temple should include political and civil leadership also. That way, there could be a total religious separation of God's people from the secular and hellenistic world. If the title of king were appropriated by the high priesthood, the separatist ideology and religious freedom to live in traditional ways could be continued. The social upheaval in the surroundings would not affect God's people.

Many influential and wealthy Jews opted for this traditionalist religious ideology. Social change could affect their personal influence as well as their religious influence. Ben Sirach is written in this preservative ideological framework which influenced the practice and meaning of temple priesthood (Sir 33, 44, 50). However, this ideology was not the only ideology of priesthood.

Many devout Jews believed that some adaptation to a world which was changing was not necessarily a compromise of the Torah. The adaptation might enhance prosperity for Palestine, and serve as a force for renewal of religious faith and custom. The living God could certainly continue to reveal the Spirit through changing times. Jews who believed that some adaptation was within the spirit of Torah, the living word of the Lord, were called hellenists. Whether hellenism was accepted or rejected by the temple priests influenced the opinions of the people.

Whichever line of priesthood controlled the temple at Jerusalem also controlled the approach taken to political and social surroundings. For example, the Maccabean priesthood stood for a clear religious separation from social changes. Thus, that line of priests favored a strong linking of civil power with the priesthood, so that a certain control could be exercised over the degree and kinds of change the Jewish people allowed. The Zadokite priesthood allowed for some adaptation to changing times, as long as the religious integrity of the people was not compromised. The Zadokites did not favor the linking of civil power with religious power as the Maccabean priesthood did. The Zadokites feared the corruption that could accompany such linking of power. Thus many Zadokite priests withdrew from the temple during, or shortly after, the time of the Maccabees. Many Zadokites joined the desert community of the Essenes, protesting the corruption of the temple and awaiting the kingdom in the desert community.[6]

In 63 b.c.e. Pompey occupied Palestine in the name of Rome. King Herod, 37 b.c.e. to 70 c.e., perceived the power of the high priests in the temple as a threat to civil order. He exterminated the temple priests of the Hasmonean line (a line of descent from the Maccabean priesthood). He also did away with lifelong tenure for the temple priests and appointed obscure persons to function as priests in the temple.

Not all the priests appointed by Herod were Herodian pawns. Some new priestly families emerged who stressed the sacred nature of the temple cult. The temple priests were put in charge of sacrificial offerings in the temple, as well as of temple revenue and taxes. At the time of Jesus Christ, the doctrinal conservatism brought the priests into favor with the Sadducees, the wealthy and powerful fundamentalists of the period. Temple priests in the common era held a great deal of power in the Sanhedrin, the religious council responsible for Jewish affairs.[7]

6. John Bright, *A History of Israel* (Philadelphia: Westminster Press, 1981) 425-62.
7. Joachim Jeremias, *Jerusalem in the Time of Jesus* (Philadelphia: Fortress Press, 1975) 170-79, 193-210.

The Lay Tradition of the Synagogue

The synagogue tradition emerged in post-exilic Israel. After the diaspora (537 b.c.e.) some Jews returned to Palestine and some did not. The synagogue was a way of gathering for both groups. The gathering was for exchanging learning, sharing in worship, reflecting upon the Word of God, and consideration of various traditions of Judaism.

The synagogue had lay leadership, not priestly leadership. Scribes, sages, rabbis, and other persons of learning and moral character, provided leadership for the various activities of the community. The prestige of the synagogue leaders did not come from a claim to either priestly lineage or hierarchical appointment. Learning, piety, compassion, and moral character set the leaders apart as models for the community.

Sometimes an entire family, like that of Hillel, became leaders in a synagogue. Such families were prominent for their wisdom and compassion. By the first century c.e. descendants of the family of Hillel comprised a major portion of the group called Pharisees. Many Pharisees were synagogue leaders. Other leaders of the synagogues came from the laity as well. Educated laity who were synagogue leaders led cultic worship, reflection upon the meaning of the Torah, and the application of Torah to the kingdom of God that was at hand. Some synagogue leaders held seats on the Sanhedrin.

At the time of Jesus Christ no synagogue leader, including the sages and rabbis, could break into the priestly caste that administered the temple. Lineage and a preservative conformity to the traditional hierarchical power structure was necessary for temple appointment. Recognizable learning and holiness were not essential, nor was the cultic ability to lead the people in prayer.

In contrast, synagogue leadership in the first century c.e. required recognizable learning, holiness, and the ability to gather the community in worship. A synagogue could exist wherever a faith community gathered and selected leadership. Leaders formed a college of elders. The college was responsible for the function of the synagogue, as well as for the structure that was needed to maintain its purpose. It is in this synagogue tradition, not the priestly temple tradition, that Jesus Christ is introduced.[8]

> He was teaching in their synagogues, and all were loud in his praise. He came to Nazareth ... and entering the synagogue ... he stood up to do the reading ... "The Spirit of the Lord is upon me ... He has sent me to bring glad tidings to the poor, to proclaim liberty to captives ... Today this scripture passage is fulfilled in your hearing." (Lk 4:15, 16, 18, 21)

This proclamation of Jesus Christ was received with hopeful expectation. "Reform your lives! The kingdom of God is at hand!" (Mt 4:17) The preaching of Jesus Christ, like the kingdom preaching of other first century religious movements, was a message the people wished to hear. A renewed fervor for the kingdom of God was evident in cultic life as well as in daily life. The blessing prayer, used in Jewish synagogues at this time, clearly stated the hopes of the people.

> Magnified and sanctified be his great name in the world that God has created according to his will. May God establish his kingdom in your lifetime, and in your day, and in the lifetime of the house of Israel, even speedily and at a near time.[9]

The kingdom was expected, but how it was to come was not a matter of agreement. Some expected the dynasty of David to be restored and Roman domination destroyed. Others expected an apocalyptic coming, a divine act of God that would usher in the kingdom. Some thought that national liberation and world transformation would simultaneously occur when God acted. Regardless of the differences about how the kingdom would come, there was a sameness in the basic concern of the period. "What must I do to enter the kingdom of God?"

8. Nathan Mitchell, *Mission and Ministry* (Wilmington: Michael Glazier, Inc., 1982) 65-70.
9. Norman Perrin, *Rediscovering the Teaching of Jesus* (London: SCM Press, 1967) 57ff.

CHAPTER 3

FIRST CENTURY RELIGIOUS MOVEMENTS

The religious movements of the first century provided a variety of answers to the kingdom question. Each movement gave its hearers an interpretation of the Torah that was slightly or greatly different from other movements. That the reign of God was linked to the people of God was agreed upon by all the movements. But there was no agreement about who would be numbered within the people of God, and what conditions there were for being the people of the new creation, the kingdom to come. The Essenes,Pharisees, Zealots, Sadducees, John the Baptist, and Jesus Christ taught of the mystery of the kingdom, how it would come, and how that kingdom could be recognized.

The Essenes

For the Essenes anyone who wished to enter the kingdom must watch, wait, and pray. The Essenes lived as a desert community. praying, fasting, and waiting for the new age. When that new age came, Israel's enemies would be destroyed in a holy war and the holy remnant would be exalted.

The Essenes perceived themselves as that holy remnant, the new temple of God. This new temple of God would replace the corrupt Jerusalem temple and its priests, who were no longer the true descendants of Abraham and the covenant. Many Zadokites, the expelled former temple priests, were members of the Essene community. Symbolically, the community chose the desert as their gathering and renewal place. In the desert, falsehood would be stripped from the harlot Israel, and God alone would renew her heart.

> Let her remove her harlotry from before her, her adultery from between her breasts, or I will strip her naked, leaving her as on the day of her birth ... So I will allure her; I will lead her into the desert and speak to her heart ... On that day, says the Lord, she shall call me "My husband" ... you shall not play the harlot or belong to any man; I in turn will wait for you. (Hos 2:4, 5, 16, 18, 3:3)

The Baptist Movement

The desert provides a comparable symbolic setting for the meaning, appearance, and proclamation of John the Baptist. The kingdom of God was indeed near, and there would be a judgment coming upon all. John "went about the entire region of the Jordan proclaiming a baptism of repentance which led to the forgiveness of sins." (Lk 3:3) The kingdom was coming soon, and those who wished to be ready must "give some evidence that you mean to reform." (Lk 3:8)

When the kingdom came, it would not be enough to claim lineage from Abraham, for "God can raise up children to Abraham from these stones." (Lk 3:8) Some wondered if perhaps John might be the messiah they awaited. John knew better.

> I am baptizing you in water, but there is one to come who is mightier than I. I am not fit to loosen his sandal strap. He will baptize you in the Holy Spirit and in fire. (Lk 3:16)

Like the Essenes, John dissociated himself and his message from the temple priesthood of wealthy conservatives. Unlike the Essenes, John preached a kingdom that would come in a less apocalyptic manner than the Essenes presumed (Mt 3). God's judgment was imminent, but there was still time for purification (Mk 3:10; Lk 3:9)

The Zealots

"What must one do to enter the kingdom of God?" The Zealots believed one must help the kingdom come about by rising against the Romans. The coming of the kingdom was in the hands of those who were willing to make it come through force, the guerrilla fighters, namely, themselves and those who would join them. Originally a sect of Galileans, their expectation for the coming of the kingdom was not an apocalyptic intervention by God. The destruction of foreign rulers by human hands would bring the freedom and liberation necessary for the people of God to live as God's people.

At the time of Jesus the Zealots were already active, and feared by some of the Romans. They stirred up the people to resist

Roman rule and to refuse paying taxes to Caesar. The new age that would usher in the kingdom of God demanded action. The action was provided by the guerrilla freedom fighters whose freedom stand would end dramatically at the Masada (73 c.e.).

The Pharisees

To enter the kingdom of God, the Pharisees taught that the people of God must be holy as God is holy. The kingdom of God would come through Israel, a priestly people. The holiness taught by the Pharisees was for everyone. The blessings of the law made holiness available through the daily life of the people.

The Pharisees were a lay group of pious Jews whose piety was strongly influenced by the piety tradition of Hillel. Traditional Jewish spirituality, living the Torah precisely, was the means to holiness. All of Torah, oral and written, must be carefully observed. There were many devout Pharisees, like Nicodemus, who did recognize the testimony of Jesus Christ during his lifetime (Jn 3). The gospel diatribes of Jesus Christ against the Pharisees must be read in the context of the second century conflicts and persecutions of Christians by Jewish authorities.

The Sadducees

The Sadducees answered the kingdom question by urging adherence to the Pentateuch of the scriptures. Halakha, the oral interpretation and ongoing creation of Torah, was not considered to be authentic Torah by the Sadducees. The questions posed by the Sadducees to Jesus indicates the traditional adherence to the Pentateuch, the books attributed to Moses.

To enter the kingdom of God, the people must observe Torah, an observance which includes paying tithes to support the Sadducees, in spite of their wealth as the aristocratic temple priests. The Sadducees had privileges which angered the country clergy who resented the difference in prestige, power, and wealth due to the temple cultic practices. The setting of the temple tax belonged to the priestly temple class, and the benefits and distribution of the cultic moneys was also their role. Understandably, they wished no change in the status quo. They remained biblical fundamentalists for they "had nothing to gain and a great deal to lose through any renewal that might challenge or alter the role of the temple in Jewish life."[10]

THE JESUS MOVEMENT: THE KINGDOM COMES

The Jesus movement was a noticeable movement. "Everyone is flocking to him," claim John's disciples (Jn 3:21). The Pharisees also noticed the popularity. "The Pharisees had heard that he was winning over and baptizing more disciples than John . . . it was not Jesus himself who baptized, but his disciples." (Jn 4:1-2) What distinguished the approach of Jesus to the kingdom of God from that of the other movements?

For Jesus, the kingdom is not a totally future reality, but a present reality that will come more fully in the future. It is this emphasis on the presence of the kingdom in the person of Jesus that provides a clear distinction from other movements and their respective kindgom proclamations.[11]

The kingdom preached by Jesus is full of surprises. The first may be last and the last may be first. Not everyone who says, "Lord, Lord" may get in or be recognized. In fact, many may enter the kingdom who never consciously acknowledged the presence of the kingdom through Jesus Christ.

> Lord, when did we see you hungry and feed you or see you thirsty and give you to drink? When did we welcome you away from home or clothe you in your nakedness? . . . I assure you, as often as you did it for one of my least, you did it for me. (Mt 25:37, 38, 40)

The kingdom preaching of Jesus was one that differed from others, for the rabbi Jesus taught "with authority and not like the scribes." (Mk 1:22) The preaching had an incarnational ring to it reminiscent of the epiphany of Jahweh in the everyday life of the Jew.

> If you forgive the faults of others, your heavenly Father will forgive you yours. If you do not forgive others, neither will your heavenly

10. Mitchell, *Mission and Ministry* 77.
11. Norman Perring, *The Kingdom of God in the Teaching of Jesus* (Philadelphia: Westminster Press, 1963) 79-80, 185-201.

Father forgive you . . . If you want to avoid judgment, stop passing judgment. (Mt 6:14, 15; 7:1)

As other rabbis and prophets before him, Jesus would summarize the Torah. "Treat others the way you would have them treat you: this sums up the law and the prophets." (Mt 7:12) The model of compassion was the heavenly Father. "You must be perfect as your heavenly Father is perfect." (Mt 5:48)

The challenge of the Torah would be sharpened by the radical proclamations of Jesus. Whoever accepted the teachings of Jesus chose to live with a kingdom imagination that went beyond the Torah as it was known at that time.

You have heard the commandment, "An eye for an eye and a tooth for a tooth." But what I say to you is: offer no resistance to injury. When a person strikes you on the right cheek, turn and offer him the other . . . You have heard the commandment: "You shall love your countryman, but hate your enemy!" My command to you is this: love your enemies, pray for your persecutors . . . (Mt 5:38, 39, 43, 44)

The proclamation of Jesus about the kingdom included not only words, but deeds. Miracles provided an important part of the message of the kingdom. Jews of the first century c.e. knew that when the reign of God came, the people of Israel would be restored to a wholeness reflective of holiness. When the kingdom of God came, the nation of Israel would be gathered, healed, and restored to a radiance befitting the people of God.

No longer will your Teacher hide himself, but with your own eyes, you shall see your Teacher. While from behind, a voice shall sound in your ears. "This is the way. Walk in it." On that day, the Lord binds up the wounds of his people. (Is 30:20, 21, 26)

The miracles of Jesus are taken out of their scriptural context if they are interpreted as actions for individuals rather than as actions of revelation for the community. That does not mean that Jesus lacked compassion for individuals. The gospels are full of statements like, "his heart was moved with pity and he cured their sick." (Mt 14:14)

But miracles, like the verbal proclamation of Jesus, were primarily for the gathering and restoring of the community. The kingdom of God was always the point of the signs. "If it is by the finger of God that I cast out demons, then the kingdom of God has come upon you." (Mt 12:28)

Israel's expectations of the gathering and restoration of the people of God had a long history of imaging. There were many lost sheep within the house of Israel. These scattered people must be gathered again as a sign for the nations. When the kingdom of God came, God would be the Shepherd who gathers and restores the lost sheep of Israel.

> Thus says the Lord God: Woe to the shepherds of Israel who have been pasturing themselves! Should not shepherds, rather, pasture sheep? You have fed off their milk, worn their wool, and slaughtered their fatlings, but the sheep you have not pastured. You did not strengthen the weak, nor heal the sick nor bind up the injured . . . bring back the strayed or seek the lost . . . I swear I am coming against these shepherds . . . I myself will pasture my sheep . . . The lost I will seek out, the strayed I will bring back, the injured I will bind, the sick I will heal. (Ez 34:2-4, 10, 15, 16)

Jesus assumes the role of shepherd. He is the gatherer of the people of God. He looks after the strays, finds the lost, and takes joy in those who are gathered around him (Mt 10). The message of Jesus Christ about the kingdom of God is addressed to all Israel. The theological composition of the hearers in both Matthew and Luke's accounts of the Sermon on the Mount makes this clear.[12]

But the disciples are also given special mention. Israel as a whole will not accept the kingdom proclamation of Jesus Christ. The disciples, and particularly "The Twelve," become the eschatological community that all of Israel was meant to be. The disciple will be the new Israel for the world, the salt of the earth, and the light of the world. When Israel became the restored and renewed people of God, all the nations were to stream toward that holy city where God was the source of light and power.

12. Gerhard Lohfink, *Jesus and Community* (Philadelphia: Fortress Press, 1984) 12-17, 35-39.

Rise up in splendor! Your light has come! The glory of the Lord shines upon you. See, darkness covers the earth and thick clouds cover the peoples. But upon you the Lord shines, and over you appears his glory! Nations shall walk by your light, and kings by your shining radiance. Raise your eyes and look about. They all gather and come to you ... For the Lord will be your light forever, and the days of your mourning shall be at an end. (Is 60:1-3, 20)

The pilgrimage of nations was a sign of the kingdom's coming. The cleansing of the temple by Jesus points to those last days. Citing Is 56:7, Mark emphasizes that the cleansing is of the court of the Gentiles. Though the cleansing of the temple by Jesus is often read as a negative statement against its misuse by the temple priests and people, the statement is more importantly a positive one. The opening of the temple of God to all peoples was an eschatological sign that the kingdom of God was already here. "My house shall be called a house of prayer for all peoples." (Mk 11:17 citing Is 56:7)

When the reign of God arrived, everything would be changed. The disciples who heard the challenge and glimpsed the mystery would give all they had to enter the kingdom. To the extent the treasure of the kingdom was found, much could be left behind.

The reign of God is like a buried treasure which a man found in a field. He hid it again, and rejoicing at his find, went and sold all he had and bought that field. Or again, the kingdom of heaven is like a merchant's search for fine pearls. When he found one really valuable pearl, he went back and put up for sale all that he had and bought it. (Mt 13:44-46)

Renunciation is not negative in following the call to the kingdom. Leaving all behind is a symbol that proclaims the reign of God changes everything. The rich young man was not able to leave all behind, so "he went away sad, for he had many possessions." (Mk 10:22) Peter, speaking for the disciples, says "We have left everything to follow you!" (Mk 10:28)

The everything is enumerated: home, brothers, sisters, mother, father, children, and property. The enormity of leaving these behind was clear to the Jews. Parents, children, brothers, sisters, and the land were all signs of blessings for the messianic age, the age of the kingdom. These were linked to the sacred portion God set aside for the people.

Jesus proclaims that the reign of God manifest in him is something the older expectations cannot contain. Those who wish to enter the kingdom of God must do the will of God. The will of God is to believe Jesus Christ and become a new family of God.

> Your mother and your brothers and sisters are outside asking for you . . . Who are my mother and my brothers? Whoever does the will of God is brother and sister and mother to me. (Mk 3:32)

In the new community of God, everything that seemed to have been left behind would be found anew. Jesus repeats the list to Peter.

> There is no one who has given up home, brothers, or sisters, mother or father, children or property, for me and for the gospel, who will not receive in this present age, a hundred times as many homes, brothers and sisters, mothers, children, and property—and persecutions besides—and in the age to come, everlasting life. (Mk 10:29-30)

In the carefully constructed parallelism of what would be left and what would be found, fathers are deliberately missing. Parallel texts provide a basis for the rather obvious omission. Mt 6:31-33 and Lk 12:29-31 proclaim that the heavenly Father knows and provides all that is necessary for life. Mt 23:8-12 urges the hearers not to give honorific titles, including father. No earthly person, however revered, is comparable to the heavenly Father, Abba. God alone is all that is necessary.

In the catechesis provided by Mt 23:8-12, a sensitivity to any symbol of domination is indicated. In the new people of God, the new Israel, the Spirit will teach all that is necessary. Whoever desires to be first, to have power, will be last.

Service, not dominating power, was the sign of the disciples who claimed the kingdom had come in Jesus Christ. As a rabbi, Jesus Christ could have the disciples serve him, for that was considered payment for the service of teaching. That practice would be changed by Jesus (Jn 13:1-20; Mk 10:45; Lk 22:27).

If the demands of the new Torah, Jesus Christ, seemed too great, there was the assurance that the burdens were light. The old Torah considered the commandments blessings, for they indicated how the people might walk in the ways of God. Jesus Christ assures his disciples that he is the way, the truth, and the light. His commands are not burdens but blessings.

But the kingdom of God would not come easily. Wherever the gospel is preached, there will be division in Israel. "Father will be split against son, and son against father; mother will be split against daughter and daughter against mother ... " (Lk 12:52, 53) Israel as a whole would not accept the proclamation of the kingdom by Jesus. Those who became disciples would have to be content with being a little flock. "Do not live in fear, little flock. It has pleased your Father to give you the kingdom." (Lk 12:32)

The disciples, together with Jesus, would be the new city of God set on a hill which could not be hidden (Mt 5:14). Compared to what was hoped for, the gathering of the scattered house of Israel, the kingdom would begin in a small way. The promised destiny would always be larger than the experienced reality. But even fragile beginnings can have surprising endings. "It (the kingdom of God) is like a mustard seed which, planted in the soil, is the smallest of all the earth's seeds ... " (Mk 4:31)

The kingdom preaching of Jesus provided a contrast to the kingdom images and teaching of the other movements. There were no national restorative tendencies in his proclamations, as there were in those of the Zealots. Unlike the Essenes, Jesus did not use images of holy wars, or of the chosen group being the only group that would inherit the kingdom. Conflicts with the temple priests and the Sadducees reflect a clear difference in opinion about the holiness of the kingdom in relationship to the Torah. The Baptist preached an imminent judgment, while Jesus preached the judgment was already manifest through those who accepted and those who rejected his teaching.

The reign of God would not fall apocalyptically from the sky. The new family of God would mediate the kingdom, but the kingdom would transcend all nations and peoples. The kingdom would not come all at once, nor would the mediating community be an ideal model of the kingdom's coming. The destiny of fulfillment that was hoped for would always loom larger than the reality that was experienced.

SUMMARY

The kingdom fervor of the first century c.e. was reflected and responded to by the variety of religious movements of that period. Each of the religious movements of the time answered the kingdom question differently. "What must I do to enter the kingdom of God?" "Repent and be baptized," said John, for the kingdom is near and judgment will be soon. "Watch, wait, fast, and pray," said the Essenes, for a holy war will ensue and the people of God will be the new temple that replaces the corrupt temple of Jerusalem. "Be holy as the Lord is holy," answered the Pharisees, for the people of God is a priestly people, a people sacred to the Lord. "Bring about the kingdom you hope to enter," claimed the Zealots, for God is surely on the side of the holy people. "Observe the Pentateuch, and do not change anything in the law of Moses," responded the Sadducees.

"What must I do to enter the kingdom of God?" "Be perfect as your heavenly Father is perfect ... Treat others the way you would have them treat you; this sums up the law and the prophets ... Love one another as I have loved you." The answers of Jesus Christ are many, but the model for entering the kingdom eventually becomes clear. "I am the way, the truth, and the life." In this kingdom community there would be a social order founded on liberating love, not on dominative power. The kingdom community would be a symbol of the new creation that all humanity was destined to become in Christ. There would be no need for a cult of the temple. Whenever the community gathered, the Lord would be in their midst. The kingdom of God would continue to come. The community gathered around the kingdom table would be a living sign of that new and eternal covenant that could inform and transform the world.

Further Thematic Development

1. Compare the symbols of temple and synagogue at the time of Jesus Christ with the contemporary meaning of temple or synagogue.

SOME SOURCES

Isenberg, Sheldon. "Power Through Temple and Torah in Greco-Roman Palestine." In *Christianity, Judaism, and Other Cults,* ed., Jacob Neusner (Leiden: Brill, 1975), vol. 2, 3:24-52:32.

Jeremias, Joachim. *Jerusalem in the Time of Jesus* (Philadelphia: Fortress Press, 1975).

Kohn, Joshua. *The Synagogue in Jewish Life* (New York: KTAV, 1973) 45-72.

Lohse, Edward. *The New Testament Environments* (Nashville: Abingdon, 1975) 146-66.

Trepp, Leo. *Judaism: Development and Life* (Belmont: Dickenson, 1974) 275-80.

2. The Pharisees had their origins in a holiness group called the Hasidim, or Pious Ones. Hasidic literature has strong similarities to Christian piety. Compare the tales, sayings, and themes of holiness to gospel parables, sayings of Jesus, and themes of holiness.

SOME SOURCES

Buber, Martin. *Hasidism and Modern Man* (New York: Harper and Row, 1958).

Mintz, Jerome. *Legends of the Hasidim* (Chicago: University of Chicago Press, 1968).

Newman, Louis. *The Hasidic Anthology: Tales and Teachings of the Hasidim* (New York: Schocken Books, 1965).

Rabinowocz, Rabbi H. *A Guide to Hassidism* (New York: T. Yoseloff, 1960).

Gospels of Matthew, Mark, Luke, John.

3. The holiness of the Essenes and the holiness of the Pharisees at the time of Jesus Christ represent two different interpretations of the same original Hasidic origin. Compare their approaches to holiness. Are there some similar strains of these two approaches in the history of Christian spirituality?

SOME SOURCES

Brown, Raymond. "Apocrypha; Dead Sea Scrolls; Other Jewish

Literature." In *Jerome Biblical Commentary,* ed. R. Brown, J. Fitzmyer, R. Murphy (Englewood Cliffs, New Jersey: Prentice-Hall, 1973) 68.83-104.

Carmignac, Jean. *Christ and the Teacher of Righteousness* (Baltimore: Helicon, 1962).

Freyne, Sean. *The World of the New Testament,* vol. 2 (Wilmington: Michael Glazier, 1980)

Lohse, Eduard. *The New Testament Environments* (Nashville: Abingdon, 1975) 74-119.

Neusner, Jacob, ed. *Christianity, Judaism, and Other Cults.*

Neusner, Jacob. *From Politics to Piety: The Emergence of Pharisaic Judaism* (Englewood Cliffs, New Jersey: Prentice-Hall, 1973).

Simon, Marcel. *Jewish Sects at the Time of Jesus* (Philadelphia: Fortress Press, 1967).

4. Contemporary Judaism in America reflects a plurality of expressions of Jewish spirituality. Contrast the Orthodox, Reform, and Conservative Jewish approaches to Sabbath observance, dietary practices, position of women. Are there some similarities to the plurality of spiritualities in Christian churches today?

SOME SOURCES

Blau, Joseph L. *Judaism in America* (Chicago: University of Chicago Press, 1976).

Neusner, Jacob. *The Life of Torah: Readings in the Jewish Religious Experience* (Belmont: Dickenson Publishing Co., 1974) 156-88.

Neusner, Jacob. *The Way of Torah* (Belmont: Wadsworth, 1979) 99-115.

Rosenthal, Gilbert S. *Four Paths to One God* (New York: Bloch, 1973) 26-212.

Trepp, Leo. *Judaism* 268-300.

Trepp, Leo. *The Complete Book of Jewish Observance* (New York: Behrman House, Inc. 1980) 156-188.

FOUR

THE FIRST FRUITS OF
THE NEW CREATION

You proclaim the death of the Lord until he comes
(1 Cor 11:26-27)

THE EARLIEST PROCLAMATION OF THE CHRISTIAN MEANING OF THE NEW creation is found in 1 Cor 11:26. "Every time, then, you eat this bread and drink this cup, you proclaim the death of the Lord until he comes!" Proclaiming the death of the Lord means living in a manner that is creative of the Body of the Lord. An authentic proclamation includes recognition that the Lord continues to be present through all people, for his love is offered to all.

Proclaiming the death of the Lord until he comes points to the future that is already known. Whenever Christians gather in memory of Jesus Christ, the past, the present, and the future come together. For the early followers of Jesus there was a familiarity with this past, present, and future dimension of the memory of God. Food was a primary symbol both of the memory and the remembering. Jesus often imaged the kingdom of God that had been promised, that was present, and that still would come, through the use of meal allusions (Mk 2:15; 6:35; Mt 8:11; 22:1-14; Lk 12:37; 22:30; Jn 2:1ff; 6; 13-15).

Food, meals, and shared tables were daily reminders that the Word of God brought life that surpassed the temporariness of food for the body. Not eating certain foods was a reminder of the covenant as well. The Jews, a people set apart to be sacred to the Lord, would remember that vocation whenever they set food apart. Such daily rituals reminded the people who they had been called to be, who they had become, and who they were yet to be in the memory of God.

In the Old Testament the memory of God for the people was a symbol of life. When God "remembered" the people, the people knew the meaning of communion with the Holy One. To remember was to "move toward" the people. If God ever turned away, or forgot the people, their existence was in jeopardy. To remember was life; to forget was death, or non-existence. If God forgot the sins of the people, the sins ceased to exist. If God remembered sins, punishment could ensue. All biblical history could be summarized through these two symbolic movements of God and the people remembering or forgetting. Remembering means there is a mutuality of presence between God and the people; forgetting means there is an absence or lack of communion.[1]

In the Old Testament there were ritual structures to help the people remember who they were and were yet to be. God provided the occasion for the memory by going with his people in bad times and good, in slavery, in exile, in restoration of their temple. Recurrent seasons, moons, stars, plantings, harvestings, light, and darkness all provided reminders of the journey of the people toward the kingdom.

For the early Christians, remembering the Lord bore similar connotations. What was done in memory of the Lord affirmed the dynamic presence of the Lord to a people he could not forget. The communion was an eternal covenant, a new covenant of memory. In this communion humans might forget, but their Lord could not. In memory of Jesus Christ the Christian communities cast christological meanings over liturgical time, and the kingdom that was celebrated within that time. Jesus Christ, the new creation, the firstborn of the dead, called the people of God to be the first fruits of the new creation.

Christian memory proclaimed that new creation whenever they gathered to eat the bread and drink the cup. Being the Body of Christ included the challenge to become the Body of Christ. Communion within the Body was a symbol of God's hope for all people. To remember was to bring God's future into the present.

1. Mary Collins, "Spirituality for a Lifetime," *Spirituality Today* 34:1 (Spring 1982) 60-65.

To forget was to eat the body and blood unworthily. Forgetting the memory that was the source of life was a sin "against the body and blood of the Lord." (1 Cor 11:27)

"You proclaim the death of the Lord until he comes" is an appeal to human freedom. The new creation in Christ calls the community to be formative of the memory, to attempt transforming history into the future of God. The Christian memory that is dynamically renewed in the eucharist critiques small-heartedness. To remember the death of the Lord until he comes is to be stirred beyond the limits of human horizons into the horizons of God. Christ has been lifted up and draws all to himself.[2]

The dynamic and life-giving memory is symbolized through the community sharing the meal of the kingdom in memory of, or in the presence of, Jesus Christ. This foundational symbol of the Christian community has both continuity and discontinuity with Jewish meals anticipating the kingdom.

This chapter will consider the memory, or presence of God, that was and is still symbolized through food and meals in Jewish and Christian traditions. First, some perspectives of the living word of God, symbolized as food in Jewish tradition, will be discussed. Second, the Christian transformation of the symbols of food, particularly the cups of Passover, will be presented. Finally, some implications of the memory of a new creation in Christ will be included in the summary of the chapter.

METAPHORS OF COVENANT MUTUALITY: FOOD, WORD, LIFE

Eating well and drinking well were symbols of an open heart, an open mouth, or open ears. The open heart, ears, or mouth all shared a common meaning. Each imbibed life from God's living word. In the Jewish scriptures, food is a symbol that is often related to the word of God. Both food and God's word mean life for the people. God's word is sweetness and delight to those who eat it, who are formed by it, who hear it, and who love it.

2. Peter E. Fink, "The Challenge of God's Koinonia," *Worship* 59:5 (September 1985) 386-403.

"Son of man," he then said to me, "Feed your belly and fill your stomach with this scroll I am giving you." I ate it and it was as sweet as honey in my mouth. (Ez 3:3)

Those who taste the word of the Lord will find joy and life. Those who spit the words out of their mouths will die. "When I found your words I devoured them; they became my joy and the happiness of my heart." (Jer 15:16) Wisdom, God's creative word, is found through participation at her table. Wisdom calls to all from "high places." Everyone should be able to hear the word spoken from "high places." No one can claim being left out of the call that is an invitation to the table.

Come, eat of my food, and drink of the wine I have mixed! Forsake foolishness that you may live; advance in the way of understanding. (Wis 9:5-6)

All you who are thirsty, come to the water! You who have no money, come! Receive grain and eat ... Heed me and you shall eat well; you shall delight in rich fare. (Is 55:1,2)

The relationship of food to the word of God is an easily understood relationship. Eating is essential for life. Hunger is an inescapable sign of the need for something more than oneself. Life is unable to be maintained in such boundaried isolation.

Hunger is the most basic experience of dependence, of contingency, of the need for others. To be hungry is to experience oneself as insufficient, as having needs, as being unable to guarantee one's own existence. To be hungry is to know in a dark, inchoate kind of way, that we do not create ourselves, but are creatures receiving our existence as gift.[3]

Those who accept their existence as gift will open their mouths wide and eat good things. Those who refuse to listen, to eat, will experience a hard or dead heart.

3. Monika K. Hellwig, *The Eucharist and the Hunger of the World* (New York: Paulist Press, 1976) 15.

If you are willing and obey, you shall eat the good things of the land. But if you refuse and resist, the sword shall consume you. (Is 1:19-20)

I, the Lord, am your God who led you forth from the land of Egypt. Open wide your mouth, and I will fill it. But my people heard not my voice . . . I gave them up to their hardness of heart. (Ps 81:11-13)

Feeding is an act of love. God's feeding of the people was a blessing, for it was a sign of communion with God. Who accepted God's food knew of an ongoing creation based in God's fidelity. The people of God passed on this food, God's word of life, to the generations to come.

Keep an omer full of manna for your descendants, that they may see what food I gave you to eat in the desert when I brought you out of the land of Egypt . . . The Israelites ate this manna for forty years. (Ex 16:33,36)

The love that is represented in the act of providing food is a constant love. Whoever prepares the table for friends is bound to stand by those who sit at that table. There is an intimate responsibility of the host or hostess for all who come to the table. God has set the pattern of this responsibility, for God is the host who sets the table of creation. When God spreads a table for the people, they can trust that the presence of their God accompanies them in all of life's circumstances. "You spread the table before me in the sight of my foes . . . Though I walk in the dark valley, I fear no evil, for you are at my side." (Ps 23:5,4)

Personification of God as shepherd, mother, and father is an image outgrowth of the symbol of food. Because God provides food and sets the table, the people know their God journeys with them and sustains their destiny. God remembers.

As a mother comforts, so will I comfort you. In Jerusalem, you will find your comfort . . . Oh, that you may suck fully of the milk of her comfort, that you may nurse with delight at her abundant breasts! (Is 66:16,11)

If feeding, and the acceptance of that food, are signs of blessing, then starving and famine are signs of judgment. When God's people forget their source of life, they have chosen the famine that comes from their lack of remembering. God brings judgment upon them to help them remember the source of life. "I will send upon them the sword, famine, and pestilence, until they have disappeared from the land." (Jer 24:10) Destruction or judgment can also come through the symbol of overindulgence, drunkenness, or gluttony.

> Thus says the Lord of hosts, the God of Israel. Drink! Become drunk and vomit! Fall, never to rise, before the sword that I will send among you . . . Howl, you shepherds, and wail! Like choice rams, you shall fall. (Jer 25:27,32)

The Lord can take away the cup of suffering or staggering as he chooses. "Hear this, O afflicted one, drunk but not with (my) wine. Thus says the Lord your master . . . See, I am taking from your hand the cup of staggering." (Is 51:22)

The people who hear and taste the word of the Lord will be fruitful people, just as vines or trees are fruitful. Those who do not hear the living word will dry up, wither, and die. They are like bad fruit, or dried up food that cannot be eaten. They have not fulfilled their creative possibilities, for they forgot the Lord. They are of little use to anyone.

> What do you see, Jeremiah? Figs, I replied . . . Thus says the Lord, the God of Israel: Like these good figs, even so will I regard with favor Judah's exiles . . . I will look after them for their good . . . I will give them a heart with which to understand that I am the Lord . . . And like the figs that are bad, so bad they cannot be eaten, even so will I treat Zedekiah, king of Judah, and his princes, the remnant of Jerusalem remaining in the land. (Jer 24:3,5-8)

The gospels show a continuity in the use of food images that would be familiar to Jewish hearers. The sayings, parables, and miracles of Jesus show the relationship of God's living word and food. Six explicit food miracles accompany, or else precede, words attributed to Jesus Christ concerning the kingdom of God (Mt 14:13-21; 15:32-39; Mk 6:34-44; 8:1-10; Lk 9:10-17; Jn 6:1-3).

The link between food and living word is made explicit throughout the gospel of John.

> I myself am the bread of life. No one who comes to me shall ever be
> hungry. No one who believes in me shall ever thirst . . . I am the
> living bread that has come down from heaven. Whoever eats this
> bread shall live forever. (Jn 6:35,51)

The food miracles have another detail that holds significance
for Jewish people. Always, there are fragments left over. God's living word is never fully heard, or "consumed" by the crowds. The
fragments left over in the food miracles are sometimes specified
as bread, but other times, presumably, include bread and fish.
Loaves and fishes provide the basic materials for the food stories
(Mt 14:13-21; 15:32-39; Mk 6:34-44; 8:1-10; Lk 9:10-17; Jn 6:1-13).
The significance of loaves as symbol of God's living word is a
more familiar symbol to Christians today than fish. But for the
Jews of the time of Jesus, fish symbols carried a kingdom significance. Leviathan, the great fish monster of the seas, was a consumer of smaller fish that humans wished to catch. Leviathan was
also a sea monster who did whatever it pleased, and thus it
became a symbol of evil. Humans, as well as other sea creatures
like fish, were helpless against this evil monster. Leviathan could
only be overcome by the Lord God. On the day of the Lord
Leviathan would be slain.

> Can you lead about Leviathan with a hook, or curb his tongue with
> a bit? Can you put a rope into his nose, or pierce through his cheek
> with a gaff? Will he then plead with you, time after time, or address
> you with tender words? . . . He regards iron as straw, and bronze as
> rotten wood. The arrow will not put him to flight. Upon the earth,
> there is not his like, intrepid he was made. All, however lofty, fear
> him. (Job 40:25-27; 41:19-20,25-26)

> On that day, the Lord will punish with his sword that is cruel, great,
> and strong, Leviathan, the fleeing serpent, Leviathan the coiled ser-
> pent, and he will slay the dragon that is in the sea. (Is 27:1)

On the day of the Lord those who had lived the law of the Lord
would consume the head of Leviathan. Another tradition claimed
that the faithful people would eat the fish as sign of the kingdom

that was brought about by God's power. The table with the food for the banquet would be set by God alone.[4] In light of this, the food miracles of the gospels, which include fish and loaves, as well as the post-resurrection meals, and the symbolic catching of fish, all bear eschatological significance. Leviathan, or evil powers of any kind, will not destroy those who remember the table set by the Lord.

For the disciples of Jesus the context of meals, like the post-resurrection meal in Jn 21, would be a familiar kingdom context. When the kingdom comes, the table will be set for all. Those who come, who remember, and who drink recognizing the Body, are the blessed of God. All disciples are called to recognize the Body, to be shepherds for each other and for all others. From those with greater direct responsibility for the community, much will be expected. There is one Good Shepherd whom other shepherds must follow.

> As a young man, you fastened your belt and went about as you pleased. But when you are older, you shall stretch out your hands and another will tie you fast, and carry you off against your will. (Jn 21:17)

The grain of wheat would have to die to bear fruit. Those who hear will yield good fruit. Those whose hearts are hard, who refuse to hear, are like dried up trees that are thrown on the fire. Fruitlessness is cursed by Jesus Christ. The fig tree event is placed side by side with the temple cleansing in Mark's gospel (Mk 11:12-21). The fruitless fig tree is cursed, the temple is cleansed, and the fig tree withers. "Never again shall you produce fruit ... Rabbi, look! The fig tree you cursed has withered up!"(Mk 11:14,21)

By contrast, the kingdom parables are often banquets associated with marriage. Marriage was a meaningful symbol of the intimacy and infinity of the God who always remembered his bride, Israel, even in the midst of infidelities. At the marriage feast in the kingdom God would prepare the table as the host. But unlike any

4. E. R. Goodenough, *Jewish Symbols in the Graeco-Roman Period* (New York: Pantheon, 1953-68), vol. 5, 37-38.

human host, this divine host would destroy all that would separate people from their God and from each other.

> On this mountain, the Lord of hosts will provide for all peoples a feast of rich food and choice wines, juicy rich food and pure, choice wines. On this mountain . . . he will destroy death forever. The Lord God will wipe away the tears from all faces. (Is 25:6-8)

Banquet images used by Jesus reflected the discipleship that would be expected around the table of the Lord (Mt 22:34-40; 25:31-46; 26:17-30; Mk 10:35-45; 14:25; Lk 14:15-23; 22:16,18,27; Jn 13, 15). Those who refuse to eat together are opposed to each other or at least have a temporarily broken relationship that cannot be healed at that time. The worst suffering or insult one can inflict on another is to eat and then betray friendship.

> Even my friend who had my trust and partook of my bread has raised his heel against me. (Ps 41:10)

> Those who eat your bread lay snares beneath you! (Ob 1:7)[5]

The food images so familiar to the Jews provide symbols of the feasting and fasting that is to characterize God's people. Both are symbols of being a people set apart for God. Fasting is a reminder of the legitimate hunger that only God can satisfy. Foods are set apart, refrained from, as memorials of identity. But food is also the symbol of the festivity involved in being a people who know the living word that is tasted as food, that is the sign of a covenant God involved with the daily journey of the people (Lv 23:27-32).

To feast and to fast were reminders of the kingdom to come. "I tell you, I will not drink of this fruit of the vine from now until the day when I drink of it new with you in my Father's reign." (Mt 26:29) The descriptions of the Lord's Supper presented in the scriptures reflect the rich food and table symbolisms of the Jewish liturgical tradition. It reflects as well the newness of table meanings because of the passion, death, and resurrection of Jesus Christ. The disciples of Christ, who knew the Easter experience of

5. Gillian Feeley Harnik, *The Lord's Table* (Philadelphia: University of Pennsylvania Press, 1981) 71-91.

a risen Lord, lived in a dynamic memory associated with a meal. This meal of memory was unlike that of the Jewish meal.[6] Its foundation was a new covenant, a new creation in, with, and through Christ.

NEW COVENANT MUTUALITY: ONE BREAD, ONE BODY, ONE LORD

Communion with God manifest through communion with the covenant community, and concern for world community were important dimensions of the Jewish covenant. The sacred meals of the Jews ritualized this covenant memory. The meal of Jesus with the disciples, referred to as the Last Supper, had this general context of meaning, though the meanings would be transformed through a new covenant.

Scholars generally agree that the Last Supper can be considered a paschal supper or Passover supper only in a very general sense.[7] That does not mean that there was not a historical meal of Jesus with the disciples. It means that the accounts of the supper are best understood in the larger framework of the passion, death, and resurrection of Jesus Christ. The accounts that are presented have been influenced by the early liturgical practices of the Christian church.

Scholars maintain that "there are no reasonable historical objections to the historicity of the Last Supper, and there is good evidence in support of its historicity."[8] At the same time, it is clear that the passion and resurrection narratives have influenced the New Testament accounts. The Lord's Supper has a basic Passover ritual structure. But the structure indicates more than a celebration of Jewish Passover with a few new meanings added.[9]

6. Reginald Fuller, *The Foundation of the Resurrection Narratives* (New York: Macmillan, 1971) 102-108.
7. Joachim Jeremias, *The Eucharistic Words of Jesus* (London: SCM Press, 1966) 41-88.
8. Howard Marshall, *Last Supper and Lord's Supper* (Grand Rapids: Eerdmans, 1980) 143. See pp. 57-75 as the basis for the conclusion reached on p. 143.
9. J. Delorme, "The Last Supper and the Pasch in the New Testament," *The Eucharist in the New Testament*, ed. J. Delorme (Baltimore: Helicon, 1963) 21-67.

A consideration of the symbolism of the cups of Passover can focus some unique dimensions of the meaning of the Christian memorial. When the supper and particularly the cups are set in context of the passion and Easter narratives, a new creation is implied. A new people of God formed by and into the Christian memory of past, present, and future have a new destiny.

CHRISTIAN TRANSFORMATION OF PASSOVER CUPS

As the Passover ritual opened, the leader blessed the day for the hope of liberation that it brought. A washing occurred at the ritual's beginning. A cup of blessing, the cup that contained the joy of Passover, was offered.

In the New Testament accounts of the supper the footwashing and the other washings mentioned in the gospels could allude to this portion of the ritual (Jn 13:2-15; Lk 22:24-27). This opening portion of the ritual served as an hors d'oeuvre part of the meal, with the main courses to follow. The announcement and departure of Judas fit in well with the ritual dippings that occurred at this time (Mt 26:20-25; Mk 14:17-21; Jn 13:21-30).[10]

In the Passover ritual a second wine cup is mixed, blessed, and the main meal is served. The question is asked: "Why is this night different from all other nights?" The Passover Haggadah, an application of the meaning of this night, would be recited by the leader. The first part of the Hillel, Psalms 113-114, occurred. Then a prayer was said over the bread. The unity of God's people is stated through the prayer over the bread. Then it is broken and distributed to those at the table. A third cup of blessing is then given to those at table.

Some commentators on the New Testament supper consider the bread broken and given and also the cup of blessing to be the elements referred to in the analogous Passover ritual action.[11] The question asked at Passover is not really asked at the Last Supper, namely, "Why is this night different from all other nights?" But for Christians the answer to the question was clear in retrospect. As

10. P. Benoit, O.P., "The Accounts of the Institution and What They Imply" in Delorme, *The Eucharist* esp. 71-80.
11. Benoit, "The Accounts of the Institution and What They Imply" in Delorme, *The Eucharist* 74; Jeremias, *The Eucharistic Words* 86.

God was liberator and life giver for the Jews, Jesus Christ would be liberator and life giver for those of the new covenant. Words attributed to Jesus provide a foundation for the new memory, the new presence of God to the people.

> This is my blood, the blood of the covenant, to be poured out in behalf of many for the forgiveness of sins. I tell you I will not drink this fruit of the vine from now until the day I drink it new with you in my Father's reign. (Mt 26:29)

The radical nature of the imperative to drink the blood of the Lord can escape contemporary readers. Jews knew that blood was not to be consumed. Blood symbolized life, and life belonged only to God. Whoever drank blood was consciously or unconsciously taking life that belonged to God alone. It was a way of acting like God, blaspheming. The punishment for that offense was clear.

> I will set my face against anyone who eats blood and will cut them off from my people. For the life of the flesh is in the blood (Lv 7:27; also see Lv 2:12; 17:10-14; Dt 12:14; Gen 9:3-5).

The response to the bread and blood discourse in John is understandable in this light of the scriptures. For Jews the drinking of blood was indeed a "hard saying." The insistence of Jesus on the matter is clear. "If you do not eat the flesh of the Son of Man and drink his blood, you have no life in you." (Jn 6:53). The Last Supper returns to this theme.

The fourth and fifth cups of the earlier ritual of Passover are not explicitly found in the accounts of the Last Supper. The fourth cup of Passover symbolized a cup of suffering. This symbol included the suffering caused by enemies which would be transformed by God, as well as acknowledgment that even enemies could be forgiven. As a ritual gesture, part of the wine in the second cup was flicked out to remember that even the suffering of enemies reduces the joy of God's people. The fourth cup was drunk after the recitation of the final part of the Hillel (Ps 114-118 or 115-118). After one drank this cup, the taste of Passover was to remain in the mouth, so no more food or drink could be taken.

Is the fourth cup of Passover, the cup of suffering, the symbolic cup that appears in the garden narratives? Such a cup was known to the people, and to the suffering servant who embodied the suffering and liberation proper to God's people (Is 42:6; 49:12; 51:17,21-23; 53). The cup of suffering is one which Jesus does not wish to drink. "Father, if it is possible, let this cup be taken away." (Jn 18:11; also Mt 26:39-44; Mk 14:36-39; Lk 22:42-44). When the cup could not be taken away, it would symbolically be drunk and the ritual forgiveness would occur. "Father, forgive them. They do not know what they are doing." (Lk 23:34)

The fifth cup of the Passover, the cup of Elijah, had a clear eschatological significance. Elijah would be the forerunner of Jahweh. Jahweh would follow Elijah and come to the temple for imminent judgment of the people (Mal 4:5ff; Eccles 48:10). By the first century c.e., Elijah had been relegated to the position of forerunner for the Davidic Messiah (Mk 9ff).[12]

At the Passover meal the fifth cup of Elijah was poured, and the door opened. This open door was a symbol of readiness for the kingdom that was yet to come. The wine would not be drunk until the kingdom came. The kingdom, like the Passover, would come at the appointed time. Elijah would also come at an appointed time.

In the pre-passion accounts of the gospels Elijah is often the topic of conversation. John sends messengers to Jesus to see if he might be the "one who is to come," namely Elijah. The response indicates to the disciples that Jesus is not Elijah, but the Messiah.

Go back and report to John what you hear and see: the blind recover their sight, cripples walk, lepers are cured, the deaf hear and see; dead men are raised to life, and the poor have the good news preached to them. (Mt 11:4-5)

Then Jesus addresses the crowd contextualizing John the Baptist in the Elijah references of the scriptures. Jesus points out that John is Elijah.

It is about this man that scripture says, "I send my messenger ahead of you to prepare your way before you" . . . If you are prepared to accept it, he is Elijah, the one who was certain to come. Heed carefully what you hear! (Mt 11:10,14-15)

12. Reginald Fuller, *The Foundations of New Testament Christology* (New York: Scribner's Sons, 1965) 43-53.

The passion accounts make various references to Elijah as well. A time of judgment, of darkness, covers the earth from noon until mid-afternoon (Mt 27:45; Lk 22:53). The outer darkness is accompanied by an inner darkness. "My God, my God! Why have you forsaken me?" (Mt 27:46; also Mk 15:53). "He is invoking Elijah! Let us see if Elijah comes to his rescue." (Mt 27:47,49; also Mk 14:36; Lk 23:37)

The link of Elijah and the kingdom is made in other ways as well. A door to the kingdom has clearly been opened. "I assure you, this day you shall be with me in paradise." (Lk 23:43) Upon the death of Jesus, "the earth quaked, boulders split, tombs opened. Many bodies of the saints who had fallen asleep were raised." (Mt 27:52-53). The cosmic terror of the last days appeared, as the temple curtain was split in two. Had Jahweh come to the temple that would be a house for all? (Is 13:9ff; 34:4)

Ironically, it is Gentiles who recognize the Lord of the temple. "The centurion and his men who were keeping watch over Jesus were terror stricken at seeing the earthquake and all that was happening and said, 'Clearly, this was the Son of God'." (Mt 27:54) The fifth cup is symbolically not drunk in some accounts, being refused by Jesus (Mt 27:48; Mk 15:36). The backdrop of Psalm 22 has influenced the story.

In John's account there is a fifth cup symbolically taken. Jesus takes the wine, then announces his life is over, and finally breathes forth the spirit (Jn 19:30). This taking of the wine of the kingdom is in accord with John's emphasis throughout the gospel. For John, Jesus Christ is the kingdom. Whoever believes in Christ has already experienced the kingdom, for it is a person, not a place.

In John the bonds of kinship are clearly beyond the natural family, for Jesus gives his mother to a friend, and the friend to be son to his mother (Jn 26-27). The kingdom family is already set forth in the synoptics as well. Whoever hears the word of God and keeps it is mother, sister, and brother. But what of the relationship of the son, Jesus, to the Father? Has there been a breaking of the kinship between the Father and Son? "My God, my God, why have you forsaken me?" (Mk 15:34) Is the radical nature of the kingdom of God parabled here as God seems to break kinship with the only begotten Son?[13]

13. Feeley-Harnik, *The Lord's Table* esp. 108-148.

Drinking the cup of Elijah is a sign that the kingdom has come. Knowing the Lord Jesus in the breaking of bread provides an early catechesis on the kingdom that has come. The liturgically influenced story of the disciples of Emmaus points to the presence of the kingdom that has come in Jesus Christ. He is the living word that is food and drink, that is the cause of "our hearts burning inside us." (Lk 24:32) The story, and others like it, can point as well to the finding of that "hidden matzah" that concluded the Passover celebration.

As the early church proclaimed the death of the Lord until he comes, there was a felt experience of the presence of Christ wherever two or more would gather. The former law required a quorum of men to constitute a gathering for prayer; the new law of Christ included men and women, two or more, to remember. In the memory, the mutual presence of the Lord and the people became alive. In the memory, there was an advent expectation of the Lord who would come in glory. The day of the Lord, the light of the new creation, was present but not fully.

Sunday became the Day of the Lord for a variety of reasons. It was the day when the Lord who had died appeared to the disciples affirming resurrection. As the community of believers went forth to meet Christ on this day, it was a going forth that was symbolic of that final day of resurrection when Christ would be all in all. Sunday was the first day, but also the "eighth day," a Jewish symbol for the "new creation" or end time. For Christians, being baptized in Christ meant being part of that new creation.[14]

The baptized members of the new family of God would walk in newness of life. This newness, connected to the kingdom, was experienced, encouraged, and guided through the community, the new family of God (Rom 6; 8:1-4; 2 Cor 5:21; Gal 3:10-14; Col 2:12-14). The old wine had been changed into a new wine, showing forth the transforming power of God (Is 55; 56; Prv 9).

As the apostles appear on Pentecost, they are ridiculed for being filled with new wine (Acts 1:2-13). The people know that new wine intoxicates. Such wine would not be found in the old

14. Geoffrey Wainwright, *Eucharist and Eschatology* (New York: Oxford University Press, 1981) 18-84. Citation of a variety of patristic texts presenting this vision of the early church can be found on p.182, n.250, n.251.

wineskins. For the Jews Pentecost was a day to remember, a day for festival. This was the day that the people celebrated receiving God's word, a word that would continue to be spoken. Peter reminds the people of the fullness they awaited as Jews, and the fullness that is present in Jesus Christ. "God has made both Lord and Messiah this Jesus whom you crucified." (Acts 2:37) What should be done by those who hear?

> You must reform and be baptized, each one of you, in the name of Jesus Christ, that your sins may be forgiven: then you will receive the gift of the Holy Spirit. (Acts 2:38)

The hope for the gathering of Israel would be symbolically achieved through the gathering of the new people of God, eventually to include Gentile as well as Jew. The ideal of the new family of God included a clear mutuality in which domination had no part. All in Christ were members of a body that was one. In that body, the new family of God, there would be no class, sex, or racial distinctions.[15] That way of life is how the community would proclaim the death of the Lord until he comes.

> All of you who have been baptized into Christ have clothed yourself with him. There does not exist among you Jew or Greek, slave or free, male or female. All are one in Christ Jesus. (Gal 3:27-28)

The ideals of the kingdom were clear enough. The dreams and visions the prophet Joel identified with the last days did appear. But like all dreams and visions, reality tempered the actual shape the dreams would assume. A tradition had been born that was continuous and discontinuous with the memory of the past. The new creation had come in Christ, but much of the old soon overpowered the new. The call to the future, "to proclaim the death of the Lord until he comes," would be a constant memory. In spite of the community's lapses into forgetfulness, the presence of the Lord through the Spirit would transform small-heartedness and shortsightedness as long as the community tried to remember.

15. Lohfink, *Jesus and Community* 39-63.

SUMMARY

The God of the Old Testament remembered the people in turning toward them in love, in forgiveness, and in punishment for their forgetfulness. When God forgot the offenses of the people, the people were forgiven. What God forgets ceases to exist. What God remembers continues to exist. So God assures the people that they will never be forgotten. God will always be willing to turn toward the people.

The people can remember God or forget God. The memory of God is inscribed into the recurrence of seasons, of new moons, of harvests and festivals. The celebration in time is not because God forgets, but because God's people can forget who they are as people sacred to the Lord. Jewish ritual provided many signs and symbols of remembering. The meal became a community reminder of the need for life given through food, through God's word. Both fasting and feasting were ways of remembering who the people are called to be for the world. God's living word, spoken to the people, is like food that sustains life, that reminds the eaters of dependence on someone besides the self. Like food, God's word is satisfying, but there will always be a need for more.

Those who remember to eat, who remember the Lord, and do not harden their hearts will be fruitful vines. Those who forget will be like dried up figs, branches fit only for being tossed on the fires. Those who know wisdom heed the invitation to come to the table. The table of the kingdom is set with rich foods and wine, and all are invited. There is an abundance of food, for the word of the Lord is never empty.

The food miracles in the gospels point to the relationship of food and God's word. There is food left over, in spite of the many people that are fed. The love of God knows no limits. The memory of God includes all. The body and blood of Christ are given for all. When the kingdom comes, all people will be in communion around the table set by Jesus Christ.

As the early church reflected upon the mystery of the passion, death, and resurrection of Jesus Christ, the Last Supper became a central memory. Death, the seal on finite existence, was not the end of the story, but the horizon of new beginnings. The new creation in Christ had come. The night "different from all other nights" would become the day different from all other days, the

Day of the Lord. The new family of God would not be limited by distinctions of class, gender, or race. The new covenant, the new memory, was a call to be and to form a new creation.

If one would not enter into the mystery of communal transformation, if one would not share what had been received, then the body .and blood of the Lord was received in vain. If anyone became too locked into the present horizon of history, the proclamation of the death of the Lord until he comes was hypocritical. The community was a necessary part of the memory that was still in process. The community in Christ would help bring the new creation, God's future, into the present.

To remember was to choose beyond small-heartedness. To remember was to live with the love of Christ that had universal horizons. To "do this" meant that there could be no barriers in the community that smacked of "forgetting" the meaning of the memory. "To proclaim the death of the Lord until he comes" meant there was one family of God, one Body of Christ.

A sense of the presence of the Spirit affirmed that the memory was true. There were soon many communities who knew the Lord Jesus in the breaking of bread, in the sharing of new wine. As those communities lived the proclamation of the death of the Lord until he would come again, diversity was normative. The next chapter will consider how different communities embraced the memory, and the basic models that gave shape to the memory as history progressed.

Further Thematic Development

1. Jewish and Christian traditions know of feasting and fasting as means of remembering as God remembers. Compare these relationships in their implications for today's world.

SOME SOURCES

Liturgy 2:1, esp. 9-13; 23-24; 45-64; 73-77.

Dussel, Enrique. "The Bread of the Eucharistic Celebration as a Sign of Justice in the Community," Concilium 152, *Can We Always Celebrate the Eucharist?*, ed., Mary Collins, David Power (New York: Seabury, 1982) 56-68.

Hellwig, Monika. *The Eucharist and the Hunger of the World* (New York: Paulist, 1976) 60-75.

Klein, Isaac. *A Guide to Jewish Religious Practice* (New York: Jewish Theological Seminary of America, 1979) 242-253.

Meehan, Francis X. *A Contemporary Social Spirituality* (New York: Orbis, 1982) 39-46.

Newman, Louis. *The Hasidic Anthology: Tales and Teachings of the Hasidim* (New York: Schocken Books, 1965) 111-113.

2. Jews and Christians have some shared vision of the meanings of covenant, Word of God, mission, and witness. Dialogue on these themes is part of contemporary Jewish-Christian relations. What similarities and differences are there in these major themes for Christians and Jews?

SOME SOURCES

Croner, Helen, and Leon Klenicki, ed. *Issues in the Jewish Christian Dialogue* (New York: Paulist Press, 1979).

Croner, Helen, and Leon Klenicki, ed. *Stepping Stones to Further Jewish-Christian Relations* (New York: Paulist Press, 1967).

Goldberg, Michael. *Jews and Christians: Getting Our Stories Straight, the Exodus and the Passion Resurrection* (New York: Abingdon, 1985).

Klein, Isaac. *A Guide to Jewish Religious Practice* 120-40.

Küng, Hans, and Walter Kasper, ed. Concilium 98 *Christians and Jews* (New York: Seabury, 1974).

Markham, Robert. "Christian and Jew Today from a Christian Theological Perspective," *Journal of Ecumenical Studies* 7:4 (Fall 1970) 744-62.

Neusner, Jacob. *The Life of Torah: Readings in the Jewish Religious Experience* (Belmont: Dickenson Publishing Co., 1974) 114-27.

Scharper, Philip, ed. *Torah and Gospel* (New York: Sheed and Ward, 1966).

Trepp, Leo. *The Complete Book of Jewish Observance* (New York: Behrman House, Inc., 1980) 168-97.

3. The tragedy of the holocaust in the twentieth century brought into clear focus the anti-Jewish sentiment that has been consistent throughout history. The roots of anti-Jewish sentiment can be

found in early Christianity. What issues has the holocaust raised for Christians who celebrate eucharist?

SOME SOURCES

Burghardt, Walter. "Jewish Christian Dialogue: Early Church versus Contemporary Christianity" in *The Dynamic in Christian Thought*, ed., Joseph Papin (Villanova, Pennsylvania: Villanova University, 1970) esp. 200ff.

Fleischner, Eva, ed. *Auschwitz: Beginning of a New Era?* (New York: KTAV, 1974).

Pawlikowski, John. "Worship After the Holocaust," *Worship* 58:4 (July 1984) 315-29; also *Responses* 330-341.

Reuther, Rosemary. *Faith and Fratricide: The Christian Theological Roots of Anti-Semitism* (New York: Seabury, 1974).

Reuther, Rosemary. "On Renewing the Revolution of the Pharisees," *Cross Currents* 20:4 (Fall 1970) 415-34.

Trepp, Leo. *Judaism: Development and Life* (Belmont: Dickenson, 1974) 153-58; 258-64.

Wiesel, Eli. *Night* (New York: Avon, 1972).

Wiesel, Eli. *A Jew Today* (New York: Vintage, 1979).

FIVE

TWO MODELS OF
CHRISTIAN WORSHIP

New wine into new wineskins
(Mk 2:22)

THE LIFE, DEATH, AND RESURRECTION OF JESUS CHRIST WAS A NEW WINE
that required new wineskins. Jesus Christ, an incarnational expression of the imagination of God, could not fit into the categories of expectation of the former law and prophets. A new covenant memory, a new experience of Emmanuel, called forth the
mystery of a new creation. The kingdom that had been awaited
had come (Mt 9:17-18; Mk 2:21-22). The dimensions and fullness
of this new wine was more than traditional wineskins could
contain.

For Christians the new wine symbolized the last days for which
they had hoped and prayed. The prayer had been answered, but
not fully, for the kindgom had not come fully. The community, the
Body of Christ, was now part of the prayer and part of the answer
for the kingdom's coming on earth as it was in heaven. All who
lived in the dynamic memory of the body and blood that was
given "for you and for all" were called to be as worldly as God.
God had so loved the world that his Son lived among its people.
Those who were baptized into this memory were called to a
worldly holiness.

The new people of God, formed in the death and resurrection
of Jesus Christ, experienced the kingdom's coming in Christ. This
new creation in Christ, the experience that the kingdom had

come, was focused in the scriptural prayer, the Our Father. Forgiveness and deliverance from eschatological evil confirmed the hope that "your kingdom come" was answered. God surprisingly broke into the present time.[1]

That new wine, the death and resurrection of Jesus Christ, made the whole earth a potential temple. The Spirit of the Lord had filled the earth! All people were invited to the communion in Christ, to Wisdom's table that was foundational to the kingdom. The Israel of the Spirit, the Body of Christ, was a visible symbol of the communion hoped for when Christ would be all in all.

This community of the new creation shared the ministry of Christ, reconciliation of all in Christ. The new temple of the Spirit, the community, was to be a holy place where there was holy egalitarianism. There would be no divisions and no privileges of estate. The gifts or charisms bestowed on the community were ordered to its communion. For "to each person, the manifestation of the Spirit is given for the common good." (1 Cor 12:7)

Purchased at a great price, the people of the new creation were slowly formed into the meaning of the new order, the new wine and new wineskins. Like all creations that include matter and form, the wineskins would eventually pose limitations for the shape and the preservation of the new wine. The early church, as the church at any era of history, functioned within a social milieu. This historical context necessarily influenced both the interpretation of the new wine and the kind of wineskins that would enhance and preserve it.

Worship in the early church exhibited a legitimate plurality of community expressions of faith. Eventually and for legitimate reasons, that worship assumed a structural uniformity. In time, the uniform worship pattern, meant to encourage a formative unity of the Body of Christ, suppressed the richness of living and faithful diversity. Whenever uniformity is imposed from outside the living and changing faith of the community, there is a danger that wineskins can preserve, but no longer enhance, the flavor of the wine.

As people, culture, and environment change, the new creation of Christ will assume new meanings. The mode of reconciliation that is most appropriate for that time and place in history may re-

1. Joachim Jeremias, *The Prayers of Jesus* (London: SCM, 1967) 66-81.

quire new wineskins. The memory that is past, present, and future, the contour and content of the meanings of that memory, will always require critical analysis by the community of memory. When the early communities gathered to "do this" in remembrance, they "remembered" in context of a particular culture, as all future communities would also remember.

The cultural milieu of the early communities made the egalitarian Christian memory a dangerous one. The memory that was ritualized proclaimed a oneness in Christ that denied the ultimacy of cultural order based on classes in society. Hierarchical measure of personal dignity and value was heretical. The divisions of rich and poor, slave and free, male and female, Jew and Gentile, powerful and powerless, were part of the surrounding Palestinian culture. However, if such divisions were brought to the table of the Lord, those who gathered were clearly not "recognizing the Body."

The community of the new creation grew from a world view that all could be one. To the extent the community understood the nature of his being and remaining Servant in and for the world, they would live in his love. Co-responsibility for the world, and for the kingdom to come into that world, set forth a world view that differed radically from the world view of the surrounding society. Worship as one Body formed and furthered the view that in Christ there could be no destructive divisions. The early church fought to keep itself free from cultural captivity that retained subtle forms of power and dignity divisions. Eventually the Christian community did succumb to some of the cultural ideologies which were slowly obscuring the Christian memory.

This is not surprising when one considers that the patterns for ordering any community are usually drawn from the familiar. The Christian community, because it is a community, follows the same anthropological norms of communal ordering as any other community. As a religious community, it will have dominant symbols that affect the way it orders, interprets, and integrates its meanings. Ritual life will enforce the values and meanings that mediate identity, form new members into the identity, and provide some continuity for future development.[2] However, in spite of its

2. Clifford Geertz, "Religion as a Cultural System," *Anthropological Approaches to the Study of Religion,* ed. Michael Banton (London: Tavistock, 1966) esp. 36-46.

uniqueness stemming from its dominant symbols, it may still borrow cultural patterns to hold and preserve its new wine. This is because cultures evolve within a world view, and religions are part of the larger context of culture.

World view is the name for the complexity of integral and foundational images, orderings, and interpretations of the reality of the community in relationship to itself and the world. World views are not simple realities. They are complex, often unconscious, and yet powerful in forming theological positions that do not easily change. World views, whether in worship, or in the larger social arena, operate in cultural boundaries. Every culture has unique intellectual and emotional mainsprings that are not, and in fact cannot, be shared fully by any other culture.[3]

From the beginnings of Christian worship, the patterns of worship, as well as the expression of the Christian memory, were both cultural and counter-cultural. The universality of the paschal mystery of Christianity was a counter-cultural proclamation. But the Christian memory throughout history is lived in cultural coordinates of time and place, and often in a shared world view reflecting that time and place.

This chapter will present the basic components of two world views that give rise to two models of interpretation and direction of human history. The models provide a basis for theological reflection and for the meanings and structure of Christian worship as well. These models will be used as windows for a comparison of an early period of Christian worship with a later medieval period of Christian worship. The limits of such a focused overview are obvious. However, the identification of such models in the history of theology can provide a foundational basis for critique of the present. They can also provide a dialogical basis for consideration of liturgical futures.

TWO WORLD VIEWS: TWO MODELS OF WORSHIP

What is a world view? A world view is a comprehensive and often unarticulated complexity of cognitive and affective perceptions of relationships. A world view affects the construction of all

3. Ruth Benedict, *Patterns of Culture* (Boston: Houghton-Mifflin, 1959) 37-52.

symbol systems that reinforce the relationships of a group to others, to time and history, and to the sacred.[4]

Many constructs contribute to the formation of a world view. From the many constructs, three interdependent elements can be identified. These elements are: organization of the relationships within a community as well as with others outside the community; a perception of the ideal, or an ideational system; a consideration of time and its historical patterning.[5]

Organization of Relationships

Social organization of relationships can be described as an adult mutuality or as a symbolic kinship. Adult mutuality presumes a basic equality that is manifest by mutual recognition, respect, and affirmative care that furthers the use of personal gifts for the community. In a community of adult mutuality each is considered responsible for the good of the community. Each adult contributes a participative perspective for the future direction of the community and the care that is necessary to promote that future. The order in the community, as well as who does what in and for the community, evolves out of community discernment. These expressions of responsible relationships differ from the other kind of communal organization which can be called symbolic kinship.

Symbolic kinship resembles the hierarchical order of familial distinctions. Symbolic parents and symbolic children have different expectations of each other, differing responsibilities for each other, and different degrees and kinds of power that can be used for better and for worse. Symbolic children have much less participation in decision making than symbolic parents. Ritual and personal leadership, responsible concern for the future of the group, and social participation in the planning that can further the life of the community reflect further differences between symbolic children and symbolic parents. There is little creativity in the

4. Dorothy Lee, *Freedom and Culture* (New Jersey: Prentice-Hall, 1959) 168-71.
5. Clifford Geertz, *The Interpretation of Cultures* (New York: Basic Books, 1973) 30-49,136-43; Marc Swartz and David Jordan, *Anthropology: Perspective on Humanity* (New York: Wiley and Sons, 1976) 48-60, 70-73, 92-96.

implementation of symbolic parental decisions. Often titles, even in adult communities, will indicate the operative model of a relational symbolic kinship.[6]

Perception of the Ideal

A perception of an ideal, an ideational system, is a second component of world views. The perception of the ideal can be expressed as idealism or empiricism. Idealism can be demonstrated through the outlook of platonic philosophy. In Platonic philosophy the ideal is a form existing apart from the knower and only partially manifest through sensible reality. The ideal is pre-existent, perfect, universal, and changeless. The heavenly is quite distinct from anything earthly. The immaterial spirit is never adequately manifest through the body or through any material object. The ideal is the spiritural, above and superior to the material.

The empricism of Aristotle provides a different approach to the ideal. The ideal is within the knower. The knower imagines, constructs, and discovers the ideal gradually through reflection upon experience. This perception of the ideal leaves room for human participation in the ultimate construction of it. Human communal behavior is both stirred and controlled by some perception of ideals.[7]

Time and History

Time can be perceived as continuous or as both continuous and discontinuous. If time is continuous or linear, the past is the basic element that measures authenticity of the present. The longer certain ways of thinking, and modes of doing occur, the more they can be trusted as sound structures for interpreting the present. The past becomes predictive of the shape of the future. If time is

6. Roger Keesing, *Kin Groups and Social Structure* (New York: Holt, Rinehart, and Winston, 1975) 9-24, 129-43.
7. Paul Kegan, *Plato's Cosmology* (London: Oxford University Press, 1937) 69.d 6-70.a 7; M. E. Opler, "Themes as Dynamic Forces in Culture," *American Journal of Sociology* 51 (1945) 198-206; G. B. Kerford, "Aristotle," *Encyclopedia of Philosophy*, vol. 1 (New York: Macmillan, 1967) 151-62.

continuous, the logical assumption is that not much changes because human nature remains the same. Time may suggest that there be some adaptation of older forms to contain some new reality. But if the past structures cannot admit the newer realities, the realities are judged as inauthentic, or deviations from the ideal.

If time is perceived as both continuous and discontinuous, the past is not predictive of the future. All that occurs in the present does not necessarily fit into the modes of doing, of perceiving, and of interpreting that have come from the past. There are moments or events in human history that are presumed to be so new in content that they cannot be explained through past structures, categories, and older perceptions. This approach to time and history allows for a new creation of forms that are appropriate to the new content of experience. There is an ease about creating a new frame of reference, for it is clear that the requirements of some periods of history require ongoing structures and forms to contain the reality. Realities that are too discontinuous with the past will not be adequately contained in any adaptation of older forms.[8]

Model One world view contains the interdependent components of symbolic kinship, an other-worldly spiritual ideal, and a perception of time and history as continuous. Order is an important value in this world view. The order is obtained through a hierarchical structure that organizes relationships, expectations, and boundaries of this community from other communities. The ideal is presumed to be better known by those symbolic parents who are higher in the ordering. The function of authority is to maintain order through preserving the past, interpreting the present, and setting forth patterns for the future that are continuous with the past. Symbolic children have little responsibility for the present or future of the community.

Model Two world view contains the interdependent components of adult mutuality, the internal but partial knowledge of the ideal, and the awareness that time is both continuous and discontinuous. This second model places responsibility for preserv-

8. Philip K. Bock, *Continuities in Psychological Anthropology* (California: Freeman and Company, 1980) 62-73, 130-33; Adolph Darlap, "Time," in *The Concise Sacramentum Mundi*, ed. Karl Rahner (New York: Seabury, 1975) 1715-20.

ing the past and creating the future within the adult community. There is a distinction in roles, but the role responsibilities proceed from communal identification of gifts, rather than from hierarchical appointment. There are no symbolic parents in this type of relational community. The community has responsibility for discerning the signs of the times and the most appropriate ways for attaining the ideals of the community. The future and its possibilities are as important in assessing the present as the study of the past. Given the discontinuous as well as continuous nature of history, this world view allows for new patterns, forms, and structures to arise. In this world view, tradition is not necessarily repetition of the past. Tradition is the life-giving source of continuity with past, present, and future meanings of this community.

Model One and Model Two can be used to focus the changing contours of Christian liturgy through its history. For the sake of comparison, an early period of Christian worship and a medieval period of worship will be focused to show the differences between the interpretation of each model. The tensions that emerge from the focus are not just past tensions. Wherever there are different underlying world views, theological reflection will manifest clear differences in interpretations of what can be judged authentically charismatic.

COMPARATIVE MODELS OF WORSHIP: TWO WINESKINS, ONE WINE

No age in Christian history has an exclusive model of worship that admits of clear separation from all elements of another model of worship. Within a universal tradition there is bound to be some plurality of expression and meaning of the mystery of Jesus Christ. This does not mean, however, that the models of worship will appear in equal proportion. For that reason there can be judgments about the dominance of one model of worship over the other at a particular time and place in history.

This section will consider two periods of Christian history and the dominant model of theologizing that characterized the life and worship of each. First, the early Christian era, approximately 30 through 100 c.e., will be interpreted. During this era the world view identified as Model Two seems a dominant model. Second, part of the medieval period, approximately 1100 through 1300 a.d., will be interpreted through the world view identified as Model One. A concluding summary will focus the comparative models of worship. This will serve as a basis for a critique of comparable models of theology operative at Vatican II, the subject of the next chapter.

EARLY CHRISTIAN WORSHIP:
MODEL TWO AND THE NEW CREATION

The new creation in Christ was not able to be contained in the imagination of the past. The Word becoming flesh, dwelling among the people and then rising from the dead, broke the horizons of expectation of religious groups of the common era. A new and eternal covenant focused the newness of this creation in Christ. The new creation was a communion in Christ, a visible symbol of the communion that all people were called to be.

For Paul the love of Christ was a challenge and an invitation to become one in communion. As one bread was broken to be received by many, the ideal for the many was to become one bread, one Body of Christ. To enter the community was to abandon the individualism of self-affirmation. "In a community which possesses the mind of Christ (1 Cor 2:16), the individual is distinguished only by different Spirit-given gifts of service (1 Cor 12:6)".[9]

This new creation in Christ had a potential universality. The eschatological gathering of Israel was already manifest through the gathering of many peoples into the one Body. When devout Jews from "every nation under heaven" gathered around the Pentecost experience of the apostles, they were "dumbfounded." "Each of us hears them speaking in our own tongue about the marvels God has accomplished." (Acts 2:5,11)

The activity of the Spirit of God affirmed the newness of this creation in Christ, the eschatological nature of the new people of God. Charisms and prophetic action characterized the whole community in the new age. In 1 Cor 14 we find the order that had to be established at worship, but this in no way destroyed the

9. Jerome Murphy-O'Connor, "Eucharist and Community in First Corinthians," *Worship* 50:5 (September 1976) 375.

charisms of the community. In the interest of corporate worship Paul insisted that gifts must be used for the good of the community.[10]

Little is really known about the precise patterns of worship of the Christian communities from 30 c.e. until approximately 60 c.e. It is the sub-apostolic period, approximately 60 c.e. until 100 c.e., in which the New Testament documents appear. Eschatology and Christology certainly shaped the worship of the early communities, but precise details are scant.[11]

What is clear is that there was an adult mutuality of relationships. The measure of the ideal was manifest through the real. The awareness that Jesus Christ had caused the end time to erupt into the present community eventually required a clear break with the past. Older wineskins could not adequately contain the new wine of Jesus Christ, the Son of God.

This general description points to the elements of a Model Two world view. This model can be evidenced through consideration of how communities viewed themselves, as well as by their attempts to function as a new creation in Christ. There was some continuity manifest in the use of Wisdom theology of the old and new covenants. The Jewish concepts of Sophia provided a basis for interpretation of the newness of Jesus Christ, particularly the universality he manifested and mediated through the new covenant.

Christ, "our Wisdom" (1 Cor 1:30), is no longer confined to Torah and temple. Christ "in you" is the community's "hope of glory." (Col 1:27) The new temple is the community, the people of God. In this temple "the manifestation of the Spirit is given for the common good." (1 Cor 12:7) The power of the Spirit leads to mutuality within the community. The greatest gift is love (1 Cor 13:13). This gift leads to the missionary horizon of the community, as well as to the unity that manifests the meaning of the Body of the Lord.

The celebration of the supper of the Lord integrates an other-

10. Hans von Campenhausen, *Ecclesiastical Authority and Spiritual Power in the Church of the First Three Centuries,* trans. J. A. Baker (Stanford: Stanford University Press, 1969) esp. 55-80.
11. Ferdinand Hahn, *The Worship of the Early Church,* trans. David Green (Philadelphia: Fortress Press, 1973) 1-5, 46-70.

wise socially stratified group of believers. Women and men, Gentiles or Jews, slave or free, are all one Body in the Lord. The Spirit gives charisms in freedom from social distinctions of nationality, gender, or social position. The source of priesthood, sacrifice, and prophecy is the community of the new creation (1 Cor 1:24,30; 3:16; 2 Cor 6:14-7:1; Col 1:15-20; Phil 2:6-ll; Eph 2:14-16,18-22; Jn l:1-14; 1 Tm 3:6). The theological understanding of this new family of God is pointed to in Gal 3:28.[12]

The community that assembled in the name of Jesus broke away from some forms and meanings of Jewish liturgy. The requirement of ten for Jewish worship now was changed to two or three gathered in the name of Jesus. Liturgical formulas borrowed from Judaism attained new significance. Amen, alleluia, hosanna, and doxologies affirmed the centrality of Jesus Christ. Eschatological rejoicing and expectation of the coming in glory were stimulants for missionary action. Specific formulas appeared alongside free prayer. Transmission of the words of Jesus and narratives concerning Jesus appear at an early date as part of Christian worship.[13]

The twofold law of love had a critical function in the first century. God's eschatological action manifest in Jesus Christ imposed itself within the community to the extent each loved in the manner of Christ. For John the relational image of disciple is primary. Who loves much can be forgiven much and can be challenged to much. Relationship in love to Jesus Christ and to the community is the point of apostolic succession. Even the presbyteral image is secondary to loving discipleship. The first and most basic question is "Do you love me?"[14] (Jn 21:15-17)

The call of the Lord to discipleship is the basis for any role anyone has in and for the community. Nationality, social status, and gender are irrelevant distinctions in the community of the beloved disciple, a community of adult mutuality. In the account of John discontinuities with the dominant cultural world view

12. Elisabeth Schüssler-Fiorenza, In *Memory of Her* (New York: Crossroad, 1984) 175-99, 221-36.

13. Hahn, *The Worship of the Early Church* 46-70.

14. Raymond Brown, *The Community of the Beloved Disciple* (New York: Paulist Press, 1979) esp. 1-20, 30-40, 60-68, 80-92.

abound. Discontinuities with some aspects of a religious world view of Judaism also abound.

It is a Samaritan woman who is the model of the ideal missionary, a missionary who points to the Lord rather than to herself (Jn 4). It is another woman, Martha, who utters a confession of faith in Jesus that other evangelists place on Peter's lips (Jn 11:27; Mt 14:33). Mary Magdalene is the first post-resurrection apostle, an apostle to the apostles proclaiming the resurrection (Jn 21).

The new creation in Christ is a creation that is discontinuous with the old creation. Love of Christ and of each other in Christ is the basis for discipleship, and for community service. The basic equality in the early Johannine communities was based upon this mutuality in Christ through the Spirit.

There is some continuity in symbols of the new creation, but the interpretations of the symbols are Christological. The first day of the new creation is set in a garden, but there is a new Adam. A woman in the garden will hear the voice of the Master and recognize it. He is alive and sends her to be an apostle to the apostles. Beyond any of the private or collective dreams of "his own," the Christ has risen.[15]

By the time the post-Pauline and pseudo-Pauline pastorals appear, there are some restrictions and interpretations about the meaning and practice of equality in Christ. The ideal of no distinctions between races, sexes, free people or slaves would be long in coming. The community of adult mutuality pointed to in the letter to the Galatians and in the Johannine writings would not last. Slowly, cultural hierarchies of communal ordering would pattern the Christian communities and their worship.

The head of the family, the paterfamilias, would be symbolically manifest in the eventual ordering of roles in worship. The Graeco-Roman patriarchal order, eventually introduced into the house churches, became theologically justified as early as the pastoral

---

15. Raymond Brown, "Roles of Women in the Fourth Gospel," *Theological Studies* 36:4 (December 1975) 688-99. The early church retained a creed on the feast of Mary Magdalene. No other woman, except the Mother of God, had a creed recited on her feast. The reason for this seems to be the consideration of Magdalene as an apostle to the apostles. The revised liturgical rubrics dropped this apostolic tribute to Magdalene.

epistles. The charisms of the Spirit in the community and the communal discernment of gifts of service in the community were soon subject to a hierarchical ordering. A curious institutionalization eventually determined who could rightly receive particular gifts for community worship and service. This was done on the basis of gender, reflecting cultural patterns of hierarchical order. In effect, this submitted the Spirit of the new creation to a cultural captivity, a captivity that placed the new wine into the human constructs of the old wineskins.[16]

In the pastoral epistles a late deutero-Pauline tradition merged with sub-apostolic traditions. In general, this could be viewed as a shift from Model Two to Model One. The charismatic functions that were the basis for communal identification of presbyters slowly became institutionalized. The appointment of leaders did not in itself lessen the prophetic possibilities of leadership within the community. The episkopos, or overseer of a community, appeared as a "first among equals" in the early church. The task was to order the community toward the kingdom of God. The early office was not linked to eucharistic presidency.

It was only when appointment was automatically linked to a supposition that appointment bestowed a teaching or didactic office apart from the discerning spirit of the community that there was a significant change. Eventually liturgical presidency would be linked to office. This does not imply that there were no prophetic or charismatic persons who held the office of presbyter or bishop. But the office was presumed to bestow the charism, rather than the charism fitting someone to be a candidate for the office.[17]

In the early church the tradition of the house churches points to the fact that there was no necessary connection made between the ministry of the presbyter and the presidency of the eucharist. In house churches the hostess or host presided (for example, Col 4:15). The New Testament assumes that whoever serves the church publicly as leader also serves the community at worship. Since the fundamental purpose of ministry is to preserve and further the ongoing identity of the new people of God, leadership

16. Schüssler-Fiorenza, *In Memory of Her* 251-79.
17. Campenhausen, *Ecclesiastical Authority* 76-80, 106ff; Hahn, *The Worship of the Early Church* 88-98.

and liturgical presidency are two faces of the same charism. There is nothing in the New Testament about any chain of sacramental power passing from Jesus to the Twelve, to missionary apostles, and then to bishops.[18]

In the first century c.e. the point of continuity and also of discontinuity is the person of Jesus Christ. It is Christ who is the two edged sword. Initially, the community of adult mutuality, of an incarnational idealism, and of an eschatological hope was a community of new wine in new wineskins. What was borrowed from the old had new meaning. What was created was legitimated by the living memory of Jesus Christ, whose truth was manifest to the community through the Spirit.

Changes in the second century already indicated a movement toward Model One, and the eventual hierarchical role of responsibility for the community. This would include the clear linking of the office of bishop to the eucharistic presidency. However, the early letters of the period still do not limit the liturgical presidency only to bishops. If Christians find themselves without clerical leaders, they may still celebrate baptism and eucharist. This practice is justified by the Christian belief about the presence of Christ. "Where there are three, even if they are laity, there is the church."[19]

By the beginning of the third century the Apostolic Tradition of Hippolytus (c. 215) indicates three distinct charisms. There are offices of presbyter, priest, and deacon. It is still the custom for the people to elect the clergy who shall lead the community and preside at liturgy.[20] This is logical given the fact that at this time, "order" refers to the entire church, the order of the new creation.

18. Raymond Brown, *Priest and Bishop* (New York: Paulist Press, 1970) 40-43; Edward Schillebeeckx, *Ministry,* trans. John Bowden (New York: Crossroad Publishing Co., 1981) 30ff.
19. Tertullian, "Exhortation to Chastity," VIII:3, quoted in Mitchell, *Mission and Ministry* 218.The link of liturgical presidency and office of bishop can be found in the letters of I Clement 40:2, 5; 44:4; The Didache 10:7, 15:1; Ignatius of Antioch to the Smyrnaeans 7:1-2. All can be found in Kirsopp Lake, *The Apostolic Fathers,* The Loeb Classical Library, vol. 1 (Cambridge: Harvard University Press, 1977) 84-85, 76-79, 260-61.
20. Hippolytus, *The Apostolic Tradition* #3-10, trans., Geoffrey Cuming, *Hippolytus: A Text for Students* (Bramcote, Notts., England: Grove Books, 1976) 9-14.

The church manifests this new order as it gathers for eucharist. Those who will gather the community and lead it into the mystery of the new creation ought to be selected by the holy order of the community.

The early history of Christian worship, with the gradual changes that occurred, indicates that the proper form of worship and the proper form of leadership in worship may be proper only to its own age in history. The new creation in Christ assumes its proper form of worship and life in the mystery of the transformation of the world in Christ. The service of Jesus Christ to the community through the Spirit is the ongoing life that empowers the community to serve the world.[21]

To remember Jesus Christ meant to proclaim by one's life the experience of life, death, and resurrection. This proclamation required a thankful remembering of all that was and would yet still be. In the present, proclamation meant "acceptance of the responsibility of prolonging the saving mission of Christ" (1 Cor 11:26). Christian remembrance is always "concerned with the past only insofar as it is constitutive of the present and a summons to the future."[22]

For Paul the bond of unity of Christians was primary. The social stratification of the communities, like the community of Corinth, was a stratification that could not be tolerated at the Lord's Supper (1 Cor 11:17-22). The Christian community must proclaim in its life what it intended to symbolize. Otherwise, in claiming to receive the Body of Christ, it might be condemned for not recognizing the Body of the Lord. All belonged to the house church as brothers and sisters, comparably loved and gifted by the same Lord.

Charismatic church order is indicative of the life and ministry in the communities of Paul. This is especially true for the communities called Romans, Galatians, and Corinthians. The authority is "free, unstructured, prophetic leadership which derives

21. Ernst Lohmeyer, *Lord of the Temple* (Edinburgh: Oliver and Boyd, 1961) 5-7, 103-5.
22. Jerome Murphy-O'Connor, "Eucharist and Community in First Corinthians," *Worship* 51:1 (January 1977) 60.

its authority from the inspiration of the Spirit and responds in an *ad hoc* manner to needs as they arise."[23]

The contrast of the charismatic nature of early Christian communities of the new creation with the stratified constructs of the medieval church is dramatic. The charismatic nature of the church was so well institutionalized by 1100 a.d. that uniformity became the measure of unity. Many factors contributed to this gradual evolution of church order from plurality to uniformity. The cultural context within which the church grew is a major contributor of the shift from Model Two to Model One.

MEDIEVAL CHRISTIAN WORSHIP: MODEL ONE AND THE NEW CREATION

Three interdependent cultural and theological themes can be simply traced between 1100 and 1300 a.d. The interdependence illustrates how a preferred world view can provide a basis for theological reflection. By 1100 the components of the Model One world view and its theological perspective were dominant. This effected a very different approach to celebration of the Lord's Supper. The three interdependent themes that contribute to the framework of theological reflection of this period are the medieval philosophy of estates, the hierarchies of Pseudo-Dionysius, and the perspective of official authority. These three themes do not exhaust the theological currents of the period, but they do provide a context for understanding how the social context of any time and place can impact upon theology.

Medieval Estates: From Holy People to Holy Order

Two basic themes of the medieval period from 1100 to 1300 influenced the perception of the people of God, including its worship. These two themes are the medieval philosophy of estates, a philosophy that ordered the society of that time; and a compatible theological construct, the Pseudo-Dionysian hierarchies. Remnants of the latter continue to operate in the church today, a point to be illustrated in the final section of this chapter.

23. Carolyn Osiek, *What Are They Saying About the Social Setting of the New Testament?* (New York: Paulist Press, 1984) 69.

The medieval philosophy of estates was operative during the eighth through fifteenth centuries. The word *estate* meant class standing. This was determined by the amount of land one owned. A person of high estate held a great deal of land. A person of low estate only held, or worked, the land for another. Bishops, most abbots, and also nobles were of the higher estate. Parish priests, friars, and commons were of lower estate.

Three classes or estates existed between 1100 and 1300 a.d. These estates were the clergy, the nobility, and the commons. Women are generally not classified by most writers, though a few put wives in the estate their husbands have. Some writers placed nuns in the estate occupied by monks or priests.[24]

The hierarchy of estates proceeded from clergy at the top to nobility to commons at the bottom. The presumption was that those at the top ought to illumine the next lower estate. These in turn illumined the lowest estate. Obedience was owed by the lower to the higher, since the higher were more enlightened. Love flowed in both directions, but responsibility and obedience were one directional.

The philosophy of estates clearly answered a basic question for medieval society. How can order be maintained and stability be assured for all? The answer was logical and simple. People are basically unequal. Order proceeds from the hierarchical arrangement of inequalities. Thus there is a legitimate hierarchy of estates that God must have intended, for God is the one who created people to be born into one or other estate.[25]

This sacralization of the order of estates, that God wanted it this way, was accompanied by other related assumptions. People would become holy to the extent they accepted and remained in their estate. If God wanted it this way, it was surely evil to try to change one's estate. The earthly order of estates ought to mirror the unchanging heavenly order. Any social uprisings would be quickly stopped by civil and church authorities because it was God's will for everyone to stay in his or her place.[26]

24. Ruth Mohl, *The Three Estates in Medieval and Renaissance Literature* (New York: Columbia University Press, 1933) 15-44.
25. Mohl, *The Three Estates* 20-44.
26. Yves Congar, "The Sacralization of Western Society in the Middle Ages," *Concilium* 47, *Sacralization and Secularization,* ed. Roger Aubert (New York: Paulist, 1969) 64-65.

The philosophy of estates provided a socio-cultural context identifiable with Model Two. Relationships were hierarchically arranged with descending power, importance, and social responsibilities. The ideal was the next world, the heavenly, and the spiritual. Surely it was not the material or the earthly. To stay in one's place and to do what the estate suggested was the way to heaven. Change destroyed the order God intended. Thus the past must provide the only legitimate models for what God wants for the present and future. The kingdom of God was not to be expected here, but only hereafter. Letting old wine remain in old wineskins was the key to the kingdom. Clearly the older the wine and the older the wineskins, the better the situation in the present. Old wine of the past is obviously superior to new wine that has not stood the test of time.

The Model One world view, foundational to the medieval philosophy of estates, was conducive to the reappearance of theological constructs known as the Pseudo-Dionysian hierarchies. In the twelfth and thirteenth centuries the hierarchies were used to interpret and to justify the distinctions between clerical and lay ministries. The ecclesiastical hierarchy was also used to justify the supremacy of papal jurisdiction and power over any and all civil power. It was the logical basis for a spirituality of priesthood that connected holiness with the separation of the priest from the material world, and from the feminine that symbolized the material world. The hierarchy of Dionysius can be seen in much canonical legislation that was codified by Gratian, including legislation that forbids women to preach to men or to teach men.[27]

The foundational suppositions of the ecclesiastical hierarchy make the conclusions understandable. There was no conscious intent of the hierarchical order to discriminate against anyone. The intent of such theological speculation was an intent that is characteristic of the church in any age. How can theological reflection

27. Mary Collins, "The Public Language of Ministry," in *Official Ministry in a New Age*, ed. James Provost (Washington, D.C.: Catholic University of America Press, 1981) 30-33; Walter Ullman, *Medieval Papalism: The Political Theories of the Medieval Canonists* (London: Methuen and Co., 1948) 90-93; Gratiani, *Decretum*, vol. 1, Causa XXIII, C. XXIX.

enable this earth to be transformed so that it more closely resembles the heavenly kingdom?

The hierarchies of Pseudo-Dionysius arrange all reality into two categories, the celestial hierarchy and the ecclesiastical hierarchy. Each hierarchy has three major divisions and three further subdivisions. A visual correspondence may enable the relationships to be more easily perceived. The categorization is as follows:

CELESTIAL HIERARCHY	ECCLESIASTICAL HIERARCHY
First Choir of Angels	*The Sacraments*
Seraphim	Eucharist
Cherubim	Unction
Thrones	Baptism
Second Choir of Angels	*Clergy*
Dominations	Bishop
Virtues	Priest
Powers	Deacon
Third Choir of Angels	*Laity*
Principalities	Monks
Archangels	Contemplatives
Angels	Penitents, Catechumens

Jesus Christ reigns over both hierarchies. He resides in the love of God and also transmits the light and love of God. This light and love of God is more proximate to the upper categories of the hierarchy.

Thus, in descending proximity, the seraphim are closest to God, praising God unceasingly. Then come the cherubim and so on. The tasks of the angels, descending from the first through third choirs, are to praise God unceasingly, to order the movement of the heavenly spheres, and to care for the earth. The guardian angels at the bottom of the categories care for the people of the earth. This clearly cannot compare in dignity with praising God.

The incarnation of Jesus Christ is not a constitutive center for either hierarchy. For Pseudo-Dionysius, the incarnate Christ is almost an embarrassment. The risen Christ must be a pure Spirit with no sexuality. This flows from the supposition that the division of the human race into sexes was a punishment for sin. If Jesus Christ was sinless, he must also be sexless.[28]

The ecclesiastical hierarchy follows a similarly descending pattern of proximity to love and light. The eucharist mediates the closest union with the Lord, the source of life and love. Other descending categories mediate life and love in accord with their particular estate. The higher estates pass on illumination to the lower and contain the illumination of the lower. The reverse does not hold true.

A threefold pattern of perfection or union, illumination, and purification imposes itself within each major category of the hierarchy. In the ecclesiastical hierarchy, bishops are the perfecting order, while monks are the order to be perfected. Priests are the illuminating order, while contemplatives are the order to be illumined. The deacons are the purifying order, while the order of catechumens and penitents are in need of purification.[29]

The higher category contains the perfection of the lower plus the illumination proper to its own class. Thus the lower could not illumine the higher, for the higher contains the illumination of the lower. Though Christian baptism does assure each of the baptized that the light and love of Christ is given, that light can only be received to the degree of one's placement in the hierarchy.[30]

From this brief description of the theological construct, it may be apparent how the distinctions between the clergy and laity came to be clarified. Clergy, the more spiritual beings, were likened to the second choir of angels. Thus clergy were closer than laity to Jesus Christ, source of light and love. The second

28. The Christology of Pseudo-Dionysius is a spiritualized Logos Christology developed in comprehensible form by Guntram Bischoff, "Dionysius the Pseudo-Areopagite: the Gnostic Myth," *The Spirituality of Western Christendom*, ed. Ellen Rosanne Elder (Kalamazoo: Cistercian Publications, 1976) 13-22, 33-40; Scotus Erigena, a translator and interpreter of the thought of Dionysius, explains the division into sexes and the connection with sin in "De Divisione Naturae," *PL* CXXII, 799, 817, 912, 981, 1003.
29. Rene Rogues, *L'Univers Dionsien* (Aubier: Ed. Montaigne, 1954) 319-29.
30. Denys Rutledge, *Cosmic Theology: The Ecclesiastical Hierarchy of Pseudo-Denys* (New York: Alba House, 1965) 11-38, 47-59.

choir of angels engaged in more spiritual functions than the third choir, for the third choir was concerned with temporal and earthly concerns. Correspondingly, the clergy should do spiritual things, while the laity should engage in temporal affairs. The decretals of Gratian were clear on the matter, and also clear about the reasons.[31]

The rise of universities in the thirteenth century raised a potential problem that the Dionysian hierarchy quickly resolved. Laity were receiving doctorates in theology, whereas many parish clergy were basically uneducated. Should that influence who can more adequately administer the sacraments?

Only the illumined ones, indicated by placement in the hierarchy, can administer sacraments. Regardless of theological education, the hierarchy makes it clear that laity, including monks, contemplatives, and converts, cannot be as illumined as clergy. The ritual of ordination certainly makes that clear.[32] The role of the laity is appropriate to their class, namely, to be busy with the temporalities and worldly mission that is precisely theirs.

During this period the power of the pope begins to be equated to the ultimate power of illumination and love that is found in Jesus Christ. The pope does not appear in the hierarchical list. However, Gregory VII (1073-1081) asked the decretalists (those who studied past decrees in the church to shed light on the present) to verify the superiority of papal power over civil power. The Dionysian construct provided a position.

Jesus Christ is the invisible head of the church, but the pope is the visible head, the vicar of Christ on earth. Canonical jurisdiction over the universal church belongs to the pope. Civil rulers have jurisdiction over specific geographical areas. Thus, papal power must be supreme if it is more universal. Since the pope is at the top of the hierarchy, he is the most proximate to the source of

31. Gratiani, *Decretum* (Romae: Typis Polyglottis Vaticanis, MCLXXXIII), vol. 1, causa XI, Q. I, C. XLVII; Donald Heintschel, *The Medieval Concept of an Ecclesiastical Office* (Washington, D.C.: Catholic University of America, 1956) 1-15.
32. The discussion of language as verification of the mythos of illumination due to office is done by Mary Collins in "The Public Language of Ministry" in Provost, *Official Ministry*, pp. 30-33. Remnants of the language remain in the revised ordination ritual today.

love and light. Rulers have lesser lights, and thus no pope needs to ask advice from the lesser luminaries.[33]

The imposition of clerical celibacy occurs in this period. It is a logical outgrowth of the Dionysian hierarchy and its emphasis on the clergy as spiritual beings. If clergy are to be likened to angels, the holy order to which they are called must be separated from passing temporalities of the earth. Sacred orders presumed a separation from the secular and the feminine. Ontological change in the ordained affirmed this change of status. Being set apart for the Lord meant being different from all others.[34]

Christian baptism into the new creation was an experience of the holy order in earlier times. By this period Christian baptism had lost its centrality to a holier order of the clergy. The liturgical life of the church, through the reforms of Gregory VII and the assistance given by the Franciscans, became clericalized as they had not been in ages past. Liturgy also became Romanized as a symbol of unity through uniformity.

The dissolution of the liturgical community was evident as the Lord's Supper became a priestly duty. The former communal recitation of the canon with its institution narrative had changed to an inaudible recitation by the priest. This was a sign of respect for the mystery, but its effect was to reduce the people to watchers. From 1000 onward, the practice of the priest's back facing the people provided a further symbolic separation of the classes in the hierarchy. Private Mass contributed to the assumption of all parts of the Mass by the presider.[35]

In one way, the Dionysian hierarchy provides a context for saying that the community was still participating in the Mass. The higher estates or classes contained the lower. Thus if a priest

33. Yves Congar, "The Historical Development of Authority," *Problems of Authority*, ed. John Murray Todd (Baltimore: Helicon, 1962) 140-156; Ullman, *Medieval Papalism* 80-97.
34. The ontological change theory is discussed clearly in an evolutionary perspective by Edward Schillebeeckx in *Ministry*, pp 70-72; canonical celibacy and concubinage legislation exist side by side in this period, and are developed by Bernard Cooke in *Ministry to Word and Sacrament* (Philadelphia: Fortress Press, 1976) 113-32.
35. Theodore Klauser, *A Short History of the Western Liturgy* (Oxford: Oxford University Press, 1979) 94-116.

prayed in the name of the people, the people were present through the priest. Stipends became symbols of the presence or care of the donor, so it really was not necessary for the donor to be physically present. The priest could pray for the designated person without anyone else being present. As private Masses increased, this is what happened with a server taking the parts of the people. A Model One world view would have no particular difficulty with this representational theology.

On the other hand, the Model Two world view, which perceives symbols less abstractly, would view such practices as a perversion of the new creation in Christ. The community was a source of the presence of the Lord. The community was called to be and to become the holy communion that was to be world transforming. When "This is my Body . . . This is my blood" is recited over objects instead of people, there is a clear confusion over who or what the Body of the Lord is.

Centuries would pass before the liturgical movement, the biblical movement, and the ecclesiological movement would renew the foundational meanings of the Body of Christ. When the return to biblical sources and historical sources of the liturgical life of the church occurred, a renewed liturgy was not far behind. The council called Vatican II would bring the renewal movements together, transforming a Model One world view into Model Two. This would eventually revitalize the Christian community by emphasizing the transforming nature of the church in and for the world.

SUMMARY

The new creation in Christ admitted of no distinctions or classes. But the new creation ideals were set within the contours of human history. In time, the familiar social patterns and world views became the normative models within which the church ordered its life. The meaning of the mystery of the Body of the Lord and the structures of that Body reflected the order that was visible in the surrounding society.

Model One and Model Two represent two outgrowths of significantly different world views. Both models have recurred throughout Christian history. Some ages have a cultural context that is more favorable to one or the other world view. Theological reflection that emanates from a particular world view will have certain limits to its vision that stem from the world view.

The contrast in dominant models of interpretation has been briefly discussed in this chapter by comparing the early church period to a segment of the medieval period. The difference in dominant theological models illustrates the influence that a social milieu can have on theological reflection.

What it means to profess the death of the Lord until he comes will be different in a Pseudo-Dionysian hierarchy construct than it will be in the framework of adult mutuality. Who has the responsibility for the community of the new creation, what gifts contribute to the order of the Body, and what futures are legitimate for the shape of the church to come vary in each model.

The coordinates for theological interpretation of the ongoing revelation of Jesus Christ will be influenced by the perception of the past. Is the past normative but not predictive of the future? Or is the past the only source of acceptable models for constructing the future? Does tradition mean that everything must have a basis in past experience? Or does tradition mean the Spirit continues to give life to the Church, and that life may come in ways that are not continuous with the structures of the past?

By the time of Vatican II, there was a discernible effect of a Model Two movement upon the worship of the Christian community. The liturgical movement had set forth principles of adult mutuality and concern for the world community. The social milieu of the world at the turn of the twentieth century provided a context for renewed reflection on what it meant to be the Body of Christ.

Liturgical and theological reflection would appear in contrasting models of the church, of liturgy, and of the church in relationship to the world and other churches at Vatican II. The differences appear side by side even in the final documents of the council. The next chapter will focus these models and the different futures possible within each mode of reflection.

Further Thematic Development

1. Theological differences between the early and medieval imaging of Christ, which in turn affects the image of the church, tends to be derived from textual sources. What can iconography of these

periods reveal about the dominant theology and faith of the people?

SOME SOURCES

Brandon, S. G. F. "Christ in Verbal and Depicted Imagery," *Christianity, Judaism, and Other Greco-Roman Cults* 164-72.
Brandon, S. G. F. *Man and God in Art and Ritual* (New York: Scribner, 1975) esp. 383-94.
Didron, Adolphe N. *Christian Iconography: Middle Ages,* 2 vols. (New York: Ungar, 1965).
Dodwell, Charles. *Painting in Europe: 800-1200* (New York: Penguin, 1971).
du Bourguet, Pierre. *Early Christian Art* (New York: Reynal and Co., 1971).
Grabar, André. *Byzantine Painting* (Geneva: Skira, 1953).
Grabar, André. *Christian Iconography* (Princeton, New Jersey: Princeton University Press, 1968).
Grabar, André. *Romanesque Painting From the Eleventh to the Thirteenth Century* (Switzerland: Skira, 1958).

2. What implications could the principle of shared responsibility in the early church hold for the church today?

SOME SOURCES

Eno, R. B. "Shared Responsibility in the Early Church," *Chicago Studies* 9:2 (Summer 1970) 129-42.
Legrand, H. M. "The Presidency of the Eucharist According to the Ancient Tradition," *Worship* 53:5 (September 1979) 413-38.
Lemaire, André. "From Services to Ministries: 'Diakonia' in the First Two Centuries," Concilium 80, *Office and Ministry in the Church,* ed. Bas van Iersel, Roland Murphy (New York: Herder, 1972) 35-49.
MacRae, G. W. "Shared Responsibility: Some N.T. Perspectives," *Chicago Studies* 9:2 (Summer 1970) 115-27.
Osiek, Carolyn. "Relation of Charism to Rights and Duties of the New Testament Church," *Official Ministry in a New Age* (Washington, D.C.: Catholic University of America, 1981) 41-59.

Power, David N. *Gifts That Differ: Lay Ministries Established and Un-established* (New York: Pueblo, 1980) 88-112.

3. Liturgical changes within the eleventh through thirteenth centuries occurred within more general cultural and theological currents. Identify some of the relationships you perceive among these currents.

SOME SOURCES

Chenu, Marie-Dominique. "Confrontation Without Schism in the Medieval Church," Concilium 88, *Polarization in the Church,* ed. Hans Kung, Walter Kasper (New York: Herder, 1973) 50-88.

Hardison, Jr., O. B. *Christian Rite and Christian Drama in the Middle Ages* (Baltimore: Hopkins, 1965).

Klauser, Theodore. *A Short History of the Western Liturgy* (New York: Oxford University Press, 1981) esp. 94-116.

Leclercq, J. "The Priesthood in the Patristic and Medieval Church," in *The Christian Priesthood,* ed. N. Lash (Denville, N.J.: Dimension, 1970) esp. 54-56.

Leclerq, J. and others, ed. *The Spirituality of the Middle Ages* (New York: Seabury, 1968) esp. 243-82, 344-72.

Van Dijk, S. J. P., and J. Walker. *The Origins of the Modern Roman Liturgy* (Westminster: Newman, 1960).

4. The theology of papal ministry in medieval society differs from the theology of papal ministry in the church of this age. What in emphasis are reflective of the different cultural and ecclesial contexts for reflection?

SOME SOURCES

Brown, Raymond. *Crises Facing the Church* (New York: Paulist Press, 1975) esp. 63-83.

Chodorow, Stanley. *Christian Political Theory—Church Politics in the Mid-Twelfth Century: The Ecclesiology of Gratian's Decretum* (California: University of California Press, 1972).

Colson, Jean. "Ecclesial Ministries and the Sacral," *Office and Ministry in the Church* 64-74.

Congar, Yves. "The Historical Development of Authority," *Prob-*

lems of Authority, ed. John Murray Todd (Baltimore: Helicon, 1962) 140-56.

Küng, Hans, ed. Concilium 64, *Papal Ministry in the Church* (New York: Herder, 1971).

Rahner, Karl. *The Shape of the Church to Come* (New York: Seabury, 1975) esp. 101-7.

Ullman, Walter. *A Short History of the Papacy in the Middle Ages* (London: Metheun, 1972).

SIX

LITURGICAL SPIRITUALITY, CONCILIAR FOUNDATIONS

All that matters is that one is created anew
(Gal 6:16)

ON 11 OCTOBER 1962 POPE JOHN XXIII OPENED VATICAN II BY ASKING THE council members to set aside the differences that would prevent the church from being created anew. The unity that was hoped for in the world could begin with the unity of renewal within the council. Pope John XXIII made a strong plea for the future. What might the church do for the unity of humanity at this point in time? After denouncing the prophets of doom, he called the assembly to proceed with hope in the task ahead.

> The Council now beginning rises in the Church like daybreak, a forerunner of most splendid light. It is now only dawn. And already at this first announcement of the rising day . . . everything here breathes sanctity and arouses great joy.[1]

Three years later on 8 December 1965 a new pope would close the twenty-first ecumenical council. Pope Paul VI would continue the hopeful vision with which Pope John XXIII began. There had been an experience of renewal for those attending the council, but the challenge of being created anew did not end there.

1. Abbott, *The Documents* 718.

This is a unique moment, a moment of incomparable significance and riches. In this universal assembly, in this privileged point of time and space, there converge together the past, the present, and the future.[2]

The dawn hoped for by John XXIII had matured into daybreak. Paul VI had the task of implementing the conciliar hopes for the future. That task proved to be a challenge of great proportions. A difficulty that had been present from the beginning continued to affect the ongoing implementation. Throughout the conciliar discussions it was evident that theological reflection was proceeding from diverse world views. Implementation of conciliar hopes also proceeded from different world views. The structures within which the reforms occurred reflect that diversity.

Using the Model One and Model Two constructs described in the previous chapter, it can be noted that there was a shift in models of theological reflection as the council progressed. The effects of three nineteenth century theological movements became more evident as the debates of the council continued. The theologies that were foundational to the biblical, liturgical, and ecclesiological movements intersected in conciliar debates. The intersection provided a firm foundation for a gradual shift from a dominant Model One theological framework toward a Model Two theological framework. The shift set forth different interpretations of the paschal mystery, and correspondingly different perspectives on ecclesiology and liturgical spirituality.

This chapter will look at the shift in models of interpretation that occurred between the beginning and end of the council. Three constitutions of Vatican II will be used as an example of the plurality of reflection that necessitated compromise in the final texts of the documents of Vatican II. What liturgical spirituality could mean for the church was influenced by the plurality of theologies evidenced in the compromised texts. What liturgical spirituality can yet mean in the future is also conditioned by the models of theological reflection.

What did Vatican II say about liturgical spirituality? Liturgical spirituality is not explictly addressed in the documents of Vatican

2. Pope Paul VI, Closing Messages to the Council, 8 December 1965, Abbott, *The Documents* 728-37.

II. However, the centrality of the paschal mystery for the Christian community is found throughout the conciliar texts and discussions. In a sense, the theology that interprets the paschal mystery and what it means for the Christian community is an essential focus of liturgical spirituality. Thus, it can be asserted that the council did address the issue of liturgical spirituality through its theologizing about the meaning of the paschal mystery.

The Constitution on the Sacred Liturgy, the Constitution on the Church, and the Constitution on the Church in the Modern World focus the meaning of the paschal mystery from different perspectives.[3] Like other theological reflections of the council, these constitutions contain a plurality of theological perspectives. This chapter will use only the constructs named Model One and Model Two to focus the reflections in the three constitutions. The focus is not intended to oversimplify complexity. Its usefulness is in providing a consistent focus that can compare the content of the three constitutions and the possible futures that emerge from using these basic models.

Using the focus provided by Model One and Model Two, the theological shift that occurred between the beginning and end of the council can be noted clearly. The first constitution to be approved, the Constitution on the Sacred Liturgy, and the final constitution that was approved, the Constitution on the Church in the Modern World, provide a striking contrast in models of reflection. Between those two accent marks of the council, the Constitution on the Church was promulgated. The three constitutions contain elements of liturgical spirituality that can be extracted from the text as well as from the context of conciliar discussions that gave rise to the texts.

Using Model One and Model Two, this chapter will focus elements of liturgical spirituality in the Constitution on the Sacred Liturgy, the Constitution on the Church, and the Constitution on the Church in the Modern World. These constitutions provide foundations for considering the renewal that has come in the past twenty years in the church. They provide as well firm foundations for future considerations that are just beginning to affect the contours of the Christian community. The focus in this chapter will be the past, the texts, the contexts, and the critiques of the final texts.

3. SC; LG; GS; Abbott, *The Documents* 137-78; 14-101; 199-308.

Later chapters will deal more directly with present and future considerations that retrospect and prospect the present to the community of the church today.

THE CONSTITUTION ON THE SACRED LITURGY

The Constitution on the Sacred Liturgy was promulgated on 4 December 1963. This constitution, promulgated early in the council, represents the earlier stages of conciliar theological reflection. These stages of reflection can be comprehended by the categories of Model One. Relationships are perceived through a framework of symbolic kinship or hierarchical ordering. The ideal is of heavenly origin, worked out, and unchanging because God is unchanging. History proceeds in a linear fashion, with past models of interpretation and action providing the normative direction for the future.

The Constitution on the Sacred Liturgy has a dominant Christology of symbolic kinship. Christ is the Son who is named sacred victim sent by the Father, sacrificed in accord with the will of the Father, raised by the Father, and given a kingdom by the Father (5, 6, 7, 12, 48, 83).

The heavenly ideal provides the pattern for earthly worship. Earthly liturgy ought to mirror the heavenly liturgy. Hymns and other forms of sacred art should reflect heavenly realities. What is human, visible, and earthly ought to be ordered to the divine, the invisible, and the heavenly (2, 8, 111, 122).

There is a linear pattern to the history of salvation. The Father sends the Son. The Son sends the Spirit. The apostles are sent to preach the gospel. The church continues the priestly work of Christ, perpetuating the sacrifice of the cross until Christ comes again (2, 5, 6, 47, 48, 83).

Continuity is assured through the hierarchical order of the church. The bishop is the high priest of the flock gathered around him, the one through whom the faithful derive and maintain their life in Christ. The clergy are directly commissioned by Jesus Christ to serve the church, while the laity are commissioned through the clergy (29, 41). The bishop is responsible for the liturgical education of the clergy, and the clergy are responsible for the liturgical education and participation of the laity (9, 12, 14, 18, 19, 41, 84, 86, 100, 129, 130). The laity are the ones for whose sake the liturgy has been made comprehensible (9, 12, 14, 18, 24, 35, 62, 63, 79, 125, 129).

Continuity is assured through the Holy See. The Roman ritual has substantial elements that may not be changed. The Holy See, or persons designated by the Holy See, will carefully see to it that any new forms of liturgical expression grow in some way from previously existing forms (22, 23, 37, 38).

The variety of commentaries on the Constitution on the Sacred Liturgy indicate both satisfaction and dissatisfaction with the final text. Those commentators who are very satisfied with the text agree with the Model One world view of divinely instituted hierarchy, the sacrificial and cultic notion of Christ's priesthood, the sacrificial nature of the Lord's Supper, and the divinely worked out linear pattern of history. Some excerpts can provide examples of these assertions.

> The Church was constituted by her divine founder after a hierarchical pattern, and in the Church, the distinct roles of those who should serve the faithful always existed, as is evident from the writings of the New Testament, and from what we know of early Christian life.[4]

The reflection that there is an objective liturgical ideal already worked out in the intent of God dominates the perspective of another commentator. The past must remain predictive of the future.

> The first law which dominates the whole concept of liturgy is the law of objectivity; the road by which we can and must go to God has not been left to man's free choice, still less to his whim. God himself has worked it out for us. Our salvation can only be accomplished if we follow that road, if we accept and adapt ourselves to God.[5]

A hierarchical approach to participation in liturgical prayer leads one commentator to assert that the difference in degrees in

---

4. Joao de Castro Engler, "The Priesthood of the Baptized Realized in the Sacred Liturgy," in *The Litugy of Vatican II,* ed. William Barauna, vol. 2 (Chicago: Franciscan Herald Press, 1966) 202.
5. N. Garrido, "Natualez de la liturgia en la Constitution liturgica del concilio Vaticano Segunda," *Liturgia* 19 (1964) 164.

participation is due to the mode of missioning of clergy and laity. Clergy are aligned with Christ, the Head, while the laity are aligned with the lower Body. Thus, clergy minister "properly and directly by virtue of ordination and laity, by virtue of the delegation of the Church, exercise a direct but delegated ministry."[6]

The degrees of participation in liturgical prayer are due to the direct will of Jesus Christ that some, namely the ordained, are granted a "full liturgical participation."[7] Others, by a comparable will of Christ, have a lesser participation.

There are commentators who are not satisfied with the final text of the Constitution on the Sacred Liturgy. Their dissatisfaction stems from the lack of an integral liturgical theology and from an inability to perceive a potential newness of liturgical possibilities. Remnants of the Pseudo-Dionysian construct remain in the distinctions of clergy and laity and the inadequate consideration of the baptismal commitment to ministry.

The commentators who critique the inadequacies of the final version of the Constitution on the Sacred Liturgy acknowledge that there are hopeful emphases as well. Christ is presented as a Lord who is present to, through, and in the community of believers. The Body of Christ is the community, who expresses and discovers its meaning through the mystery of the eucharist (2, 7, 10, 12, 14, 48, 49, 83, 99, 104, 106). There is clearly a responsibility for participation in the liturgical life of the church (7, 11, 14, 26, 37, 48, 64, 78, 83, 99). Yet a basic link is missing between liturgy and world transformation.[8]

There is an inadequate treatment of the relationship and differences between pious practices and liturgical prayer. What is it that makes prayer "liturgical"? Is it the community who con-

6. Salvator Famosa, "De sacrae liturgicae instauratione," *Ephemerides Liturgicae* LXXVIII: Fasc. III-IV (1964) 259.
7. Engler, "The Priesthood of the Baptized," in Barauna, *The Liturgy of Vatican II* 111.
8. Joseph Lecuyer, "Liturgical Assembly: Biblical and Patristic Foundations," Concilium 12, *The Church Worships,* ed. Johannes Wagner and Heinrich Rennings (New York: Paulist Press, 1966) 3-18; Cypriano Vagaggini, "Fundamental Ideas of the Constitution," in Barauna, *The Liturgy of Vatican II* 120-28; Mary D. Collins, "Eucharistic Proclamation," *Worship* 41:9 (November 1967) esp. 538-41.

sciously gathers in the name of Christ? Is it the content and form of prayer? Is it appropriate leadership? Or is it essentially approval by the proper authorities who decide what is and what is not "liturgical prayer"? On the one hand, certain adaptations of the fixed liturgy of the hours is considered "liturgical." Even a private, rather than communal, recitation of an approved form of the liturgy of hours is considered "liturgical." On the other hand, a community can consciously gather in the name of Christ, and still be engaging in a pious practice that is not liturgical prayer. Does that in fact mean that the essential issue is approval of the Holy See?[9]

Certain presuppositions about liturgical prayer disturb some commentators. First, there is a concern for renewal and adaptation of the liturgy of the hours. But two things are notoriously missing in this concern. First, an apostolic clergy may need to pray in a form more appropriate to their ministerial life. Second, there is no room for admitting new forms of prayer that could emerge from communities of laity and religious. The liturgy of the hours seems to be the only prayer form that can be called liturgical even if it is celebrated privately! New forms emerging from life experience of praying communities are not encouraged.[10]

There is an inconsistency in the constitution that is manifest in the explicitly stated principle that all Christians have a right and responsibility to participate in the sacramental life of the church (6, 10, 14, 26, 59, 83). However, the reality of the situation is that at least half of the Christians in the world have no way of frequently participating in the Lord's Supper. Though this is clearly a detriment to the foundational mystery of the new creation in Christ, no viable options were presented. The theological assumption is that

9. Josef Jungmann, "Liturgy, Devotions, and the Bishop," Concilium 2, *The Church and the Liturgy*, ed. Johannes Wagner (New York: Paulist Press, 1965) 151-58; Josef Jungmann, "A Great Gift of God to the Church," in Barauna, *The Liturgy of Vatican II* 65-70.

10. Josef Jungmann, "Constitution on the Sacred Liturgy," *Commentary on the Documents of Vatican II*, vol. 1, ed. Herbert Vorgrimler (New York: Herder, 1967) 1-13; C. J. Walsh, "Authority, Initiative, and Responsibility," *Life and Worship* 172 (October 1972) 1-8; Jungmann, "A Great Gift of God to the Church," in Barauna, *The Liturgy of Vatican II* esp. 70.

the communities of the church are formed into the paschal mystery, the living memory. Yet no mention is made of the right to the eucharist that could be exercised if broader interpretation of sacramental ministries were implemented. To provide such access to the sacrament of eucharist is a responsibility of a church that continues to baptize.[11]

Part of the difficulty in addressing such issues as the above is the linking of apostolic succession to the hierarchy of bishops rather than to the whole church. If the whole community were considered as receivers of the Spirit, the community would be the source of identification of needs, ministers, and ministries to meet those needs. The meaning of active participation in the liturgical life of the church would assume a different meaning than is presently the case.[12]

The present interpretation of the hierarchical ordering of the church and of the liturgy does not allow for the emergence of new forms of prayer and presidency. In some cases the ideal that is presented for the liturgical celebration of the community is not a possibility for the majority of the church. For example, the bishop is considered the liturgical leader of the diocese around whom the people gather for eucharist. Priests are the symbolic extension of the bishop. The fact is, for many people, that the bishop is liturgically invisible, and the priest is the symbol of Christ, not of the bishop.[13]

There is a need for hierarchical approval of the slightest change made by a priest. There is a hierarchy of instruments, the organ being more sacred than others. There is a sacred music, chant, that is preferable to other forms. There is mention of training choir

11. Peter Kearney, "New Testament Incentives for a Different Ecclesial Order?" Concilium 80, *Office and Ministry in the Church,* ed. Bas van Iersel and Roland Murphy (New York: Herder and Herder, 1979) 58-63; Edward Schillebeeckx, "The Christian Community and Its Office Bearers," Concilium 133, *The Right of the Community to a Priest,* ed. J. Metz and E. Schillebeeckx (New York: Seabury, 1980) 126-34.
12. Johannes Remmers, "Apostolic Succession: An Attribute of the Church," Concilium 34, *Apostolic Succession,* ed. Hans Küng (New York: Paulist Press, 1968) esp. 37-51.
13. Joseph Pascher, "Relationship Between Bishop and Priests According to the Liturgy Constitution," Concilium 2, *The Church and the Liturgy,* ed. Johannes Wagner 28-31.

boys, but not girls, perhaps with a similar sacrality implied (114, 116, 117, 120).

In summary, this second set of commentaries reflects a disappointment with the lack of creative possibilities in the finished text. If the past alone remains predictive and normative of the future, much of the Christian church will be celebrating liturgies of the Word but not of Sacrament. Anthropological and human sciences ought to have some impact on the liturgical reforms for tomorrow's communities of faith. This is an ever-present responsibility of the church.[14] It can be speculated that a different text would have been produced if this were the last text of the council rather than the first. At the same time, it is evident that the discussions accompanying the liturgy constitution affected the text of the Constitution on the Church, so the end result of theological reflection may not have been similar regardless of the order of the constitutions.

THE CONSTITUTION ON THE CHURCH

The Constitution on the Church was unanimously approved and promulgated on 21 November 1964. The discussions that occurred between the first schema and the final text indicated a plurality of understanding that necessitated certain compromises in the text. Some of these issues and discussions will be focused in this section to provide a context for understanding the presence of both Model One and Model Two throughout the finished text.[15]

An issue that arose early in the discussions about the church was the relationship between charism and hierarchy. The differences in the council can be summarized through two representative persons. Leon Cardinal Suenens maintained that "each

14. Heinrich Rennings, "What Is Liturgy Supposed to Do?", Concilium 42, *The Crisis of Liturgical Reform*, ed. Johannes Wagner and Heinrich Rennings (New York: Paulist, 1969) 130–37.
15. The most comprehensive source of the presentations, discussions, suggestions for change, disagreements, and voting that provided the church with the documents of Vatican II is the *Acta Synodalia Sacrosancti Concilii Oecumenici Vaticani Secundi*, 6 vols. (Romae: Typis Polyglottis Vaticanis, MCMLXXI-MCMLXXVI). References to this collection will be noted as *Acta*.

and every Christian has a charism in daily life, but as St. Paul says, 'All of these must aim at one thing, to build up the Church'."[16] Ernesto Cardinal Ruffini maintained that all charisms come through the hierarchy of the church, and are ordered by them.[17] Where the emphasis is placed makes a basic difference in constructing any theology of the church, any theology of what is or is not "liturgical," and any theology of holiness.

The council discussed at length the fact that there is a universal call to holiness implicit in Christian baptism. The Constitution on the Sacred Liturgy had grounded all Christian vocations in the corporate holiness of the church. Thus, former phrases like "states of perfection" apply to all Christian vocations. All vocations bear witness to the kingdom of God, the eschaton.[18] In spite of the rather long discussion affirming that all vocations bear witness to the eschaton, religious life is still set apart as a "better" witness to the final age. In context of the discussions, the "better" is clearly linked to virginity.[19]

Two reasons account for the conclusion. The risen Christ is apparently presumed to be sexless, or transcendent to sexuality. This was the presentation that Pseudo-Dionysius maintained, male and female being the result of sin. Discussion of the kind of body that the body of resurrection will be has a long history of sexless interpretation which will not be detailed here.

The second presupposition of the undivided heart of virgins and celibates can be more simply contextualized. For varieties of reasons, Christian tradition has linked physical virginity with a more wholehearted love of Christ than conjugal love of marriage suggests. The stoicism that has accompanied much of the ecclesial interpretation of sexual intimacy certainly contributed to that notion. Theologies that are suspicious of matter in general, and feminine matter in particular, such as that represented in the Pseudo-Dionysian hierarchies, made further contributions. Such notions are biblically erroneous as well as theologically unfounded.

Biblically, the virgins who follow the Lamb (Christ) in the

16. Suenens, *Acta*, vol. 2, pars III, 176.
17. Ruffini, *Acta*, vol. 2, pars II, esp. 617-30.
18. Elchinger, *Acta*, vol. 2, pars III, 389-90; Huyghe, *Acta*, vol. 2, pars III, 646-49; Leger, *Acta*, vol. 2, pars III, 632-33.
19. Ziade, Butler, *Acta*, vol. 3, pars I, 389-91, 420-21.

Apocalypse are symbolic of all Christians, and all people, whose lives were lived under the love command of Jesus Christ. The followers are Christians of all walks of life. Theologically, the Constitution on the Church clearly maintains that all Christians are called to the fullness of holiness. The "undivided heart," that integral love of Christ that directs all other loves, could be expected of all Christians, married and unmarried. It can be hoped, however, that such traditions of discriminatory expectations will eventually die in the more authentic Christian tradition of the universality of the call to holiness.

The council did affirm that the missionary nature of the Christian vocation presumes that all of the baptized are called to be world transformers. This was to be done in a manner appropriate to one's vocation.[20] However, the council reflected great differences of opinion on what was "appropriate" for laity and what was not. Some felt that a strong and unwarranted paternalism dominated the discussions. This was evidenced in the language of the discussions, as well as in the hierarchical control over charismatic possibilities for the future.[21]

There was extended discussion about the potential expansion of ministries of the laity and of the clergy. The pastoral responsibility of all Christians for each other and for the world was affirmed. However, there were great fears and deep confusions that surfaced in the discussions. The confusion and fear that arose was particularly manifest in those who could conceive of the future only through patterns of the past. The discussions of such crucial topics eventually ceased as emotions ran too high.[22]

A variety of discussions occurred around the issue of the relationship of the Roman Catholic Church to other Christian churches. Some members of the council strongly asserted that the universality of the paschal mystery was the source of the universality or catholicity of the Roman church. The universality of the

20. Rugambwa, *Acta,* vol. 2, pars I, 368-70; Rastouil, *Acta,* vol. 2, pars III, 10-15.
21. de Smedt, *Acta,* vol. 2, pars IV, 142-44; Leger, *Acta,* vol. 3, pars II, 219-22; Elchinger, *Acta,* vol. 1, pars IV, 147-48.
22. Ricketts, *Acta,* vol. 2, pars II, 314-17; Suenens, *Acta,* vol. 2, pars II, 317-20; Siri, *Acta,* vol. 2, pars II, 572-73; Schroeffer, *Acta,* vol. 2, pars III, 70-74; Martin, *Acta,* vol. 2, pars III, 377-80.

paschal mystery is greater than the visible manifestation of it through the Roman Catholic Church. Another way of stating the same thing is to say that the Mystical Body of Christ is larger than the Roman Catholic expression of it. Though most agreed to these general statements, many at the council still insisted that the Roman Catholic Church possesses a fullness of truth which other churches do not have. Other ecclesial groups could share in that fullness of truth to the extent they are in communion with the Roman church.[23]

The Constitution on the Church was a document that was in process for some time. The many discussions that preceded the final text reflect a difference in world views that affect the kind of theological reflection that was possible. Both Model One and Model Two remain side by side in the final text. The compromises are apparent when the text is organized through the elements of the two models.

A Model One Christology remains in some portions of the text. The victim Christ, who once gave his life in obedience to the Father, now is at the right hand of the Father. The earthly exile of Christ is finally over (6, 8, 28, 36, 37).

The continuity in the plan of salvation is evidenced through apostolic succession of the hierarchy of the church (7, 19, 20, 24). A synopsis of the hierarchy makes it clear that there are distinct roles, responsibilities, and power appropriate to every level. The language used to describe this is often reminiscent of the language of the Dionysian hierarchy.

The pope has "full, supreme, and universal power over the Church and he must always exercise this power fully" (22). That power must be acknowledged and submitted to "even when he (the pope) is not speaking ex cathedra" (25). Infallibility resides in the office of pope, but it is also "individually present" in the person (25). Infallibility resides in the body of bishops when they, with the pope, exercise teaching authority (25). By omission, infallibility cannot reside in the universal body of bishops if they are not in agreement with the pope.

The bishop channels "the fullness of Christ's holiness in many ways and abundantly" (26). The bishop has "fullness of orders"

23. Carli, *Acta,* vol. 1, pars IV, 158-61; Huyghe, *Acta,* vol. 1, pars IV, 195-97.

and can give individuals different degrees of participation in the church (28). Bishops "have succeeded to the place of the apostles as shepherds of the Church" (20). Priests have not been theologically likened to "shepherd" in the text, in spite of the fact that they are named "pastor" (shepherd).

Priests "in a certain sense" make the bishop present to the laity (28). Priests are dependendent upon the bishop, are "aids and instruments" of the episcopal order, and are aligned with Christ, the head of the Body. Priests should "look upon the bishop as their father and reverently obey him. And let the bishop regard his priests ... as sons and friends" (28).

"At the lower level of the hierarchy are deacons" dedicated to works of love, administration, and worship, according to the bishop's design (29). The laity come next on the hierarchy. They share in the priestly, prophetic, and kingly mission of Christ. The laity, "with ready Christian obedience," should "accept whatever their sacred pastors, as representatives of Christ, decree in their role as teachers and rulers in the church" (37).

Pastors should consider the suggestions of "competent" laity "with fatherly love"; the suggestions should come from the laity only "through the agencies set up by the Church for this purpose" (37). Laity have "the capacity to be deputed by the hierarchy to exercise certain church functions" (31, 33, 36). However, generally the laity should spread the kingdom of God through their work in the world and not in the church.

The final text acknowledges that everyone is called to a fullness of holiness, but holiness shines out in "a particularly appropriate way . . . in the practice of the counsels customarily called evangelical" (39). Religious vocation is "a better symbol [than marriage?] of the unbreakable link between Christ and his Spouse, the Church" (50). It is better because "it foretells the resurrected state and the glory of the heavenly kingdom . . . with particular accuracy" (50). Religious institutes are under "proper patriarchal authorities" who must approve modifications in rule, customs, and practices.

These examples of Model One categories in the final text can be joined by comparable examples of Model Two categories. The mutuality of Jesus Christ with the disciples is the model for the mutuality within the Christian community. The loving power of the Lord, experienced by the community, is meant to be shared with all people. Christians, called to the fullness of holiness, must be world transformers in the name of Christ, regardless of the cost (1, 5, 8, 9, 11, 12, 13, 19, 20, 24, 28, 33, 36, 38, 40, 41, 42, 51).

Christian holiness has a corporate context, for salvation is mediated through the community. Yet there is always a call to holiness that addresses individual uniqueness. The Christian community consists of varieties of gifts that build the Body of Christ. All are called to be informed by and formers of the kingdom of God. No vocation is "holier" than any other, for the church is a church of holiness and sinfulness (11, 30, 32, 34, 35, 36, 38, 41, 42, 51).

The vocation of the church is to foster communion with all people. The paschal mystery provides the model for the universal love to which the church is called. The Spirit touches the heart of everyone (8, 11, 15, 16, 35, 36, 41, 42, 51).

Though many more examples could be given of Model One and Model Two, the examples seem sufficient to indicate the plurality of world views operative in the conciliar discussions and in this text. Commentators are quick to point out that the Constitution on the Church, in spite of the plurality of theologies, represents a significant shift in the theology of the church. The emphasis on the church as communion in Christ provides a complement to the hierarchical emphasis assumed at Vatican I. The universality of the call to holiness eliminates distinctions furthered by language like "states of perfection." Other Christian communities are acknowledged as ecclesial bodies. All of this makes the constitution one of the key documents of the council.[24]

THE CONSTITUTION ON THE CHURCH
IN THE MODERN WORLD

The Constitution on the Church in the Modern World was approved on 19 November 1965. The constitution had been in process for five years. The final text reflects a consideration of over

24. *Vatican II: The Constitution on the Church,* ed. Kevin McNamara (Chicago: Franciscan Herald Press, 1968); *One, Holy, Catholic, and Apostolic,* ed. Herbert Vorgrimler (London: Sheed and Ward, 1968); *Commentary on the Documents of Vatican II,* ed. Herbert Vorgrimler and others, vol. 1 (New York: Herder, 1967) 105-284.

twenty thousand suggestions from the conciliar body. It shows as well the later theological reflection of the council.

One commentator identifies four major themes that give a consistent theological foundation for the variety of issues addressed by the constitution. First, the universality of the paschal mystery provides the context for the church's embrace of all humankind in Christ. Second, if Jesus Christ is the beginning, end, and focal point of human history, then the secular order can contribute to a new creation in Christ while it maintains its legitimate autonomy. Third, the universality of the paschal mystery means that Jesus Christ can be known through, but not fully contained in, each culture. Finally, there is an ambiguity in both the world and church because both know of sin and redemption. A theme that was more clearly developed in earlier versions of the text was an explicit relationship between liturgical celebration and world transformation.[25]

The Constitution on the Church in the Modern World strongly reflects a consistent Model Two view of relationships, time, and ideal. By the incarnation, Jesus Christ "has united himself in some fashion with everyone," and the Spirit offers everyone the possibility of being associated with the paschal mystery (22).

This universal mutuality of Jesus Christ provides the basis for the universality of the Christian community (1, 3, 6, 10, 11, 18, 22, 24, 32, 41, 45, 78). In a number of ways, the constitution states that the mission of the church is to care for the world (92). The community, not individuals, mediates the kingdom of God. The transformation of all in Christ requires a community (21, 22, 27, 28, 41, 92). The church may join in communion with other groups who share the hope for justice, dignity of all, and freedom (11, 16, 36, 40, 42, 43, 44, 45, 55).

The transformation of the world is at the heart of the celebration of the eucharist (38). All forms of discrimination, any form of injustice or oppression, must be consciously changed by the Christian community. The primary duty of the community is to further unity through alleviation of discrimination, including injustices in its own institution (29, 30, 35, 36, 38, 41, 42, 58, 59, 60, 83-87).

25. Charles Moeller, "History of the Constitution," in Vorgrimler, *Commentary on the Documents*, vol. 5 (New York: Herder, 1969) 1-14, 30-41, 68-76.

The new age of history makes some older patterns of perception inadequate (4, 7, 8, 58, 61, 69). Dangers as well as exciting possibilities are inherent in the technological powers available in this age. For the first time in history, there is the possibility of communication and development of a universal culture (61). All Christians have a responsibility to exercise care and leadership in the rapidly changing world so that greater communion among peoples of the world results (30, 38, 39, 40, 42, 45, 53, 55, 70).

Commentators look to this constitution as one which embraces a responsible adulthood of the community. Christians are called to assume responsibility for the world, for they have a consciousness of Christ whose life is given for all. The creative design of God for human history, centered in Christ, has called Christians to embrace all people as God's people. The church, the universal sacrament of salvation, is the community who works toward the new creation through transforming this world. These more global perspectives have yet to affect the kind of symbols used in liturgical celebration, or the form and content of liturgical prayer. The potential universality of the Body of Christ could be more adequately symbolized. [26]

Having considered three constitutions in summary form, there can be two ways to look at liturgical spirituality. If the Model One World view and the theology that flows from it are the focal mode for interpretation, liturgical spirituality can be engendered through hierarchical ordering, communal obedience and love of Christ attested to by obedience to the hierarchy, a centrality of the bishop as chief liturgist in the church and the main source of the community's growth in Christ, and a care to preserve and foster those forms of the past that are predictive and normative for the future. The paschal mystery is central to faith, but some of the baptized may not have direct access to that central mystery if the structures of eucharistic presidency limit it to seminary trained ordinands. In such cases, a lesser appointee may perform some

---

26. M. D. Chenu, "Anthropologie de la Liturgie," *La Liturgie Après Vatican II, Unam Sanctam* 66 (Paris: Editions du Cerf, 1967) 158-66, 171-77; Johannes Feiner, "Particular and Universal Saving History," in *One, Holy, Catholic, Apostolic,* ed. Herbert Vorgrimler (London: Sheed and Ward, 1968) 163-80, 192-206.

related sacramental blessings, and in some instances, sacraments, but not the central mystery of the faith.

If Model Two is used as the focus for interpretation of the liturgical spirituality that may evolve in the shape of the church to come, a different set of presumptions occurs. The needs of the community affect which ministries need to be performed, and who the community may discern to perform them. The Spirit of Christ is continuity for the church. The Spirit may suggest new modes of ministry whose patterns are not found in the past. Theological legitimacy for new patterns of sacramental ministry, presidency of the eucharist, and so on may be found in the past. But the structures may have to come forth from the present and future needs of the church. This leads to a different emphasis of every Christian being called to holiness as a minister in some form appropriate to vocational call. Model Two suggests a different set of traditional expectations for the kingdom of God that is to come than Model One suggests.

SUMMARY

The three constitutions discussed in this chapter point to a difference in world views underlying conciliar reflections. The Constitution on the Sacred Liturgy shows a predominance of Model One interpretation of the church and its liturgical life. The later Constitution on the Church reflects a mixture of models. The final constitution, the Constitution on the Church in the Modern World, reflects a Model Two interpretation. If the final constitution can be taken as normative for its interpretation of the pashcal mystery, liturgical spirituality could be summarized in the following way.

First, liturgical spirituality is formed and informed by the paschal mystery of Jesus Christ. That mystery is a mystery of communion experienced in the church, the Body of Christ. To "do this in memory of me" is a life-long challenge to the church to be mediator and former of the new creation in Christ. What that means for a liturgy that uses more universal symbols for East and West, male and female, believer and unbeliever, without loss of traditional symbols has yet to be worked out.

The celebration of the Lord's Supper is a living memory that empowers the community to do the truth it celebrates, to be the community it is called to be without discrimination of class, vocation, gender, ethnicity, and race. What that means in terms of the Christ present in the heart of every person and culture has only begun to be explored. The Roman model of liturgical life is a monocultural model. The mission of the church today is to become as universal in liturgical form and practice as its theology is in theory. Different cultural eyes and changing historical coordinates may provide the foundation for the church being created anew in this age.

The living of the Christian memory, to care for all people, was linked to the celebration of universal love that the Lord's Supper clearly focuses. The Constitution on the Church made it clear that all Christians are called to the fullness of holiness, to love as Christ loves. The Constitution on the Sacred Liturgy made it clear that Christ loves all, and gave his life for all. In the liturgy Christ continues the transformation of all people, of all of life, through and with his Body, the church.

Contemporary liturgical spirituality bears some similarities to that of the early church whose life and hope reflect a Model Two interpretation of community, reality, and history. The similarities are found in the adult mutuality that reaches beyond the Christian community to the world. Who can be called ecclesial bodies was described by the Constitution on the Church. But who can celebrate and share in the liturgy of the Body of Christ is not always congruent with who is nominally called the Body of Christ.

The kingdom of God has come in Christ. It is this earth that is the starting point for the mediation of the kingdom of God. Particular circumstances in history will affect how the kingdom is best mediated to that time and place. The mystery of Christ is always an incarnational reality that the Spirit guides. If the Spirit is continuity, then new practices more fitting for the present and future memory of Christ may still appear within the tradtition. It is the future of God, not the future of past practices, that is normative for the memory.

The world of the twentieth century is a technological world. The human power that can transform or destroy that world is a source of great hope and of great fear. Knowledge of human life is scientifically greater than at any prior age. Psychological knowledge of human love is consciously organized as it has not been in ages past. Thus, the Christian community today will proclaim the death of the Lord until he comes in many cultural contexts of slavery, compulsions, and freedoms.

There cannot be a turning back to the simpler times of past ages in a nostalgic attempt to recreate what cannot be translated into present conditions. The liturgical spirituality of the early church cannot be relived in the same way, for the Christian memory has added meaning and content in the centuries past. The evolution of sacramental meaning cannot reverse itself. The evolution of global development cannot look to earlier and simpler times, to earlier world views to contain the reality of today.

Liturgical spirituality looks instead to the memory that holds the promise of the future as well the meaning of the past and present. In the future the kingdom of God shall come in fullness. But it is in the present that we plan for and anticipate the future. The present includes historical and cultural conditioning of the Christian memory. Twenty years after the close of Vatican II, the implications of indigenization are still in need of investigation. The next chapter will address that issue in context of North American cultural experience.

Further Thematic Development

1. Vatican II renewed an earlier theology of laity in the church. Since Vatican II, what further theologies have developed about the gifts and responsibilities of laity in the church?

SOME SOURCES

Boff, Leonardo. "Is the Distinction Between Ecclesia Docens and Ecclesia Discens Justified? Concilium 148, *Who Has the Say in the Church?*, ed. Hans Küng, Jürgen Moltmann (New York: Seabury, 1981) 47-51.

Govaart-Halkes, Tine. "In Search of New Forms of Authority and Obedience in the Church," Concilium 49, *Secularization and Spirituality,* ed. C. Duquoc (New York: Paulist Press, 1969) 69-82.

Kung, Hans. "Participation of the Laity in Church Leadership and Church Elections," *Bishops and People,* ed. Leonard and Arlene Swidler (Philadelphia: Westminster, 1970) 87-112.

O'Meara, Thomas. *Theology of Ministry* (New York: Paulist Press, 1983) 3-25, 134-75.
Power, David N. *Gifts That Differ: Lay Ministries Established and Unestablished* (New York: Pueblo, 1980) 59-87.
Schillebeeckx, E. *Ministry: Leadership in the Church of Jesus Christ* (New York: Crossroads, 1981) 136-42.
Vidales, Paul. "Charisms and Political Actions," Concilium 109, *Charisms in the Church,* ed. C. Duquoc, C. Floristan (New York: Seabury, 1978) 67-77.

2. The charismatic and institutional nature of the church was affirmed by Vatican II. What are some necessary tensions that contemporary theologians see between these two emphases of the living church today?

SOME SOURCES

Duquoc, Christian. "Charism as the Social Expression of the Unpredictable Nature of Grace," *Charisms in the Church* 87-96.
McDonnell, K., ed. *Presence, Power, and Praise: Documents on the Charismatic Renewal,* vol. 3 (Collegeville: The Liturgical Press, 1980) esp. "Theological and Pastoral Orientations on the Cathic Charismatic Renewal: Malines Document I."
Power, David N. *Gifts That Differ* 36-56.
Provost, James. "The Catholic Church and Dissent," Concilium 158, *The Right to Dissent,* ed. Hans Küng, Jürgen Moltmann (New York: Seabury, 1982) 13-18.
Sartori, Luigi. "The Structure of Juridic and Charismatic Power in the Christian Community," *Charisms in the Church* 56-66.

3. The Constitution on the Sacred Liturgy emphasized the centrality of the eucharist as formative and expressive of the church. What questions must be addressed if the right of the baptized to the eucharist is to be honored today?

SOME SOURCES

Collins, Mary. "Obstacles to Liturgical Creativity," Concilium 162, *Liturgy: A Creative Tradition* (New York: Seabury, 1983) 19-26.
Kearney, Peter. "New Testament Incentives for a Different Ec-

clesial Order," Concilium 80, *Office and Ministry in the Church* (New York: Seabury, 1972) 50-63.

O'Meara, Thomas. *Theology of Ministry* 176-207.

Power, David N. "The Basis for Official Ministry in the Church," *Official Ministry in a New Age* (Washington, D.C.: Catholic University of America, 1981) 60-88.

Provost, James. "Toward a Renewed Canonical Understanding of Official Ministry," *Official Ministry in a New Age,* 194-255.

Rahner, Karl. *The Shape of the Church to Come* (New York: Seabury, 1975) 82-89, 108-18.

Schillebeeckx, E., and J. B. Metz, ed. Concilium 133, *The Right of the Community to a Priest* (New York: Seabury, 1980).

4. Vatican II emphasized the universality of the call to holiness. Critically look at the prayers of the sacramentary as well as the revised baptismal rites to find illustrations of this expectation. What theology of universality do you find in the prayer texts?

SOME SOURCES

Rites, vols. 1, 2.
Sacramentary.

SEVEN

CHRISTIAN MEMORY AND
LIFE DIRECTION

Do this in memory of me
(1 Cor 11:25)

CHRISTIANS ARE A COMMUNITY OF LIVING MEMORY. LIKE OTHER COM-
munities of memory, Christians tell the story of the memory that
is their origin and source of ongoing identity. Like other communities of memory, Christians ritualize and interpret anew the
meanings of the memory. Like other communities of memory, the
Christian community realizes its meaning is embedded within a
foundational past, a meaningful present, and a hoped for future.

Unlike other communities of memory, the Christian community celebrates a living Lord who is the memory. That living
presence is known through the ritual breaking of bread, as well as
through the less conscious ritual of touching others, or being
touched by them. Liturgical spirituality as a source of life direction
is based in this consciousness of living all of life "in memory
of me." To "do this" is no easy task. "Lord, when did we see you
hungry and feed you ... welcome you away from home ... As
often as you did it for one of these, you did it for me." (Mt 25:37-
40).

The Christian memory, centered in the One whose life was
for the many, is at once infinite and intimate. It is infinite insofar as
the embrace of Jesus Christ is "for you and for all."

It is intimate insofar as the daily "ordinary" is the context for experiencing the extraordinary.

As the Gospel of John clearly relates, the mutuality inherent in the memory challenges the community to give freely what has been received. Mutuality, not role distinctions, titles, or primacy of position within the community, is the key for living into and creating the memory anew. A meaning of the memory that is the source of this new creation is acted out by Jesus. The new creation is not like the expectations of the old. "Do you wash my feet? . . . do you understand what I just did for you? . . . There is no greater love than this: to lay down one's life for one's friends" (Jn 13:8,12; 15:12, 13).[1]

The lifelong pilgrimage toward that liberation is both focused and renewed around the table of the Lord. The community of memory gathers to embrace the universality and particularity of the Christian mystery of faith. To "do this in memory of me " calls forth an active contemplation. The community of memory prays for the kingdom to come, and for a deliverance from illusions of false kingdoms that appear when the memory is partially forgotten.

The remnants of an old creation die slowly and hard. This is one reason why the community must continually gather in the living memory of the kingdom yet to come. The community of memory celebrates a dangerous memory, for the challenge of change is embedded within it. To proclaim the death of the Lord until he comes is to consciously transform one's own portion of the world into an environment of justice and peace. For the Christian community, eucharistic mysticism is always an active contemplation.

> Authentic contemplation, through the encounter with the Absolute God, leads to the absolute love of one's neighbor. Authentic Christian contemplation, passing through the desert, transforms contemplatives into prophets and heroes of commitment, and militants into mystics.[2]

1. Sandra Schneiders, "The Footwashing (Jn. 13:1-20): An Experiment in Hermeneutics," *Catholic Biblical Quarterly* 43:1 (January 1981) 76-80, 89-92.
2. Segundo Galilea, "Liberation as an Encounter with Politics and Contemplation," Concilium 164, *The Mystical and Political Dimensions of Christian Faith,* ed. Claude Geffré and Gustavo Gutierrez (New York: Herder, 1974, 1974) 28.

Handing on the tradition that has been received requires a sensitivity to the particular forms of social sin that are preventing the new creation from appearing. There will be a plurality of arrangements of meanings of the memory, for the nature of social and ecclesial illusions differs from place to place and time to time. This was already evident by the sub-apostolic era. Handing on the tradition necessarily assumed different shapes and different structures to meet the needs of the various communities of memory.[3]

Twentieth-century America provides a unique cultural context for handing on the memory. A dimension of technological universality invites the world to be as visually close as a television channel. A visual awareness of the abusive and transformative possibilities of power can awaken new meanings of the universality of the Christian memory.

In a more global technological setting the universal church has come to this awareness of the paschal mystery.[4] "Since Christ died for all," Christians "ought to believe that the Holy Spirit in a manner known only to God offers to everyone the possibility of being associated with this paschal mystery."[5] The paschal mystery assures those who believe that universal community is not "a hopeless cause," but that love known and shared "in the ordinary circumstances of life" is a beginning of a greater community.[6] The global proportions of community are not ignored. Christians are encouraged to promote justice, peace, and dignity on an international scale when it is possible.[7] The kingdom of God does not proclaim a kingdom unrelated to this world. "On this earth, the kingdom is already present in mystery."[8]

The liturgical life of the church focuses the universality and particularity of the memory. Liturgy is "the outstanding means by which the faithful can express in their lives, and manifest to others, the mystery of Christ and the real nature of the true

---

3. *The Churches the Apostles Left Behind* esp. 19-30.
4. GS 19-22, 27, 28, 38-40, 43, 93; Abbott, *The Documents* 215-22, 226-27, 235-39, 242-44, 307-8.
5. GS 22; Abbott, *The Documents* 222.
6. GS 38; Abbott, *The Documents* 236.
7. GS 30, 35, 41, 88; Abbott, *The Documents* 228-9, 233, 240, 302-3.
8. GS 39; Abbott, *The Documents* 237.

church."[9] One sign of the true church of Christian memory is the manifestation of "the special obligation" to "make ourselves the neighbor of absolutely every person."[10]

The Christian community ritually celebrating the personal and universal meanings of the memory is the community that must keep the memory alive. A critical and creative consciousness is necessary to hand on the tradition that serves as a constant corrective for all forms of oppression and for all forms of cultural captivity of the church. Until all people are reconciled in Christ, the fullness of the sacramentality of the world will not be accomplished.

Christian memory is based in the sacramentality of Jesus Christ, a God with us as one. When that humanity of Jesus Christ is lost in favor of divinity, "we may eventually forget not only the humanity of Jesus but everyone's humanity, including our own." When that happens, "we may forget the whole social nature of Christianity in favor of a vague, cosmic religion of pure spirit which tries to go directly to the godhead."[11]

It is the community of memory, shaped by the intimacy and infinity ritualized in the eucharistic mystery, that is the locus and critic of the future of the tradition. But the Christian community of memory necessarily resides in a cultural community of memory. This chapter and the final chapter will consider some past and present aspects of the North American cultural community within which the Christian community of memory functions. Each community has some shared dreams and visions, but also some different dreams and visions. Each community has heroic figures who embody certain manifestations of those dreams and visions. Both communities of memory share a common hope for the future that is contained in the ideals of the memory that gave birth to the community. All of this is part of a tradition that both communities of memory attempt to understand, and in understanding, become renewed in the meanings.

9. SC 21 Abbott, *The Documents* 137.
10. GS 27; Abbott, *The Documents* 226-7.
11. William Johnston, *Christian Mysticism Today* (San Francisco: Harper and Row, 1984) 94.

THE AMERICAN COMMUNITY OF MEMORY

The American community of recorded memory emerged from a clear biblical piety. Those who represented a new exodus into a promised land arrived in the new Jerusalem with high ideals and shared dreams. This new American dream would eventually be given clear expression.

> We hold these truths to be self-evident: that all people are created equal; that they are endowed by their Creator with certain inalienable rights; that among these are life, liberty, and the pursuit of happiness ... whenever any government becomes destructive of these ends, it is the right of the people to alter, or to abolish it, and to institute a new government.[12]

The characteristic independence of the new nation was not an ideal that came simply. Thirteen colonies would have to become a community if the ideals were to be protected and nourished. Only a community could see to it that the rights to liberty and justice were preserved. Because God was the source of the inalienable rights, any nation or ruler that tried to take away the rights was against God. Anarchy could be holy, a work of God through the people of manifest destiny.

> Three millions of people armed in the holy cause of liberty ... shall not fight our battles alone. There is a just God who presides over the destinies of Nations and who will raise up friends to fight our battles for us ... Is life so dear or peace so sweet as to be purchased at the price of chains and slavery? Forbid it Almighty God! I know not what course others may take; but as for me, give me liberty or give me death.[13]

The American community of memory, with its inherent contours of dignity and justice for all, strongly supported the rights of individuals. On the other hand, individuals had to be willing to

12. The Declaration of Independence, 4 July 1776, in *101 Famous Poems*, ed. Roy J. Cook (Chicago: Regnery, 1958) 178.
13. Patrick Henry, "The War Inevitable," March 1775, in Cook, *101 Famous Poems* 177.

sacrifice for the sake of the community. Early historical documents point to the balance between individual and communal rights and responsibilities.

> We must be willing to abridge ourselves of our superfluities, for the supply of other's necessities ... We must delight in each other, make other's conditions our own, rejoice together, always having before our eyes our community as members of the same Body ... The eyes of all people are upon us, so that if we shall deal falsely with our God in this work we have undertaken ... we shall open the mouths of enemies to speak evil of the ways of God.[14].

There is a unique tension in the evolution of American piety. The biblical perspectives of the community in Christ, with its accompanying devotional piety, has grown up side by side with a utilitarian individualism. Though Puritanism and utilitarianism have collapsed as viable extrinsic shapers of American culture, the inner remnants of both continue to inform the American psyche.[15]

On the one hand, there still remains a sacredness of the individual, at least in theoretical ideals. Dignity, liberty, and justice for each person is assured through the constitution. Biblical individualism places the sacredness of the individual in the mystery of God manifest in and through the human community. But utilitarian individualism places the individual and the community in relationship to each other only insofar as it is useful. A modern ideology of individualism places the individual alone as the center of reality. This form of individualism cannot support any community or society because of the premise upon which it is based. If the individual is the measure of reality, there will be social collapse. Inalienable rights cannot survive without some form of community attachment. The tension between individual and community relationships has affected the churches in America. Do the churches exist only because individuals come together to make a church a visible community? Or does the church exist prior to individuals, and act as a leavening force to help individuals come to

14. John Winthrop, "A Model of Christian Charity," *Winthrop Papers II, 1623-1630* (Boston: Massachusetts Historical Society, 1931) 295.
15. *The New Religious Consciousness,* ed. Charles Glock and Robert N. Bellah (Berkeley: University of California Press, 1976) 333-66.

communal responsibilities? How do individual freedom and communal responsibility mutually enforce each other in God?[16]

The ambivalence of individualism and community appears in a larger cultural context than the churches represent. American mythic heroines and heroes are a fascinating blend of utilitarian individualism and biblical social concerns. On the one hand, the American heroic image projects the autonomous loner whose value comes through marginality with any community. On the other hand, some American communities of memory tell stories of heroes and heroines who are active transformers of the religious or civic community and remain within the heart of the community.

Examples of the first type of hero or heroine fill American folk literature. The rugged individualism, and even the naming of some heroes, for example, "The Lone Ranger," portrays the embodiment of moral courage and autonomy. The guardian of the community must remain his own person, unknown and invulnerable. "Who is that masked man?" the communities may ask. No answer is forthcoming. Knowing the person behind the mask would strip the hero of his mystery and power. Batman and Robin are also masked, for somehow, they too are less effective if they are known. For Clark Kent, or Superman (I, II, III), relationships must be very carefully monitored. A costume of another kind sets Superman apart from the daily persona. His weakness is linked to an inanimate object, krypton. In each case evil will prosper as the weakness inherent in personal identity is discovered.

Shane, Emerson, Thoreau at Waldon Pond, and a host of others, reflect another face of American independence and sacred space. Inner space as well as outer space must be protected from unwelcome intrusion. Being one's own person means living within chosen, sacred spaces. Such journeying may be done most fruitfully without being "tied down" to the dependency needs of another. Early and later heroes of this type make a collective and unique statement about American mythos.[17]

16. *Habits of the Heart*, ed. Robert N. Bellah and others (Berkeley: University of California, 1984) 142-48, 243-48.
17. John C. Cawelti, *Adventure, Mystery, and Romance: Formual Stories as Art and Popular Culture* (Chicago: University of Chicago Press, 1976); Leslie Fiedler, *Love and Death in the American Novel* (New York: Stein and Day, 1966).

This brand of American individualism is not necessarily selfishness. Society can be served well by those who must stand alone. But there are contrasting heroes and heroines who serve society well by being deeply related to those they serve. American communities of memory know of this type of heroism as well. John Winthrop, Anne Hutchinson, Sojourner Truth, Abraham Lincoln, Susan B. Anthony, Elizabeth Cady Stanton, Martin Luther King, Jr., Dorothy Day, Tom Dooley, John and Robert Kennedy, represent this form of mythos. Heroism means staying at the heart of a community, attempting to transform what can be transformed. For such heroes and heroines self-reliance and autonomy have little meaning apart from social commitment. If the commitment is situated within a Christian commitment, there is not a wish to destroy all enemies, but a wish to have enemies transformed.

> When the underprivileged demand freedom, the privileged first react with bitterness and resistance . . . the non-violent approach does not immediately change the heart of the oppressor. It first does something to the hearts of those committed to it . . . finally, it reaches the opponent . . . and reconciliation becomes a reality.[18]

The superstars of real or of TV life provide another facet of American heroic imaging. Detectives, police, and medical superstars are the new symbols of communal commitment. Perry Mason, Mike Hammer, Jessica Fletcher, Serpico, Scarecrow and Mrs. King, Policewoman, T. J. Hooker, Airwolf, Trapper John, M.D., the Hill Street Blues, Lady Blue, Magnum P.I., Simon and Simon, and a host of others fill in prime time. These television heroes and heroines serve the community, usually with little or no remuneration that can compare with the humanitarian service each provides.

Real life superstars, the athletic heroes and heroines, the Hollywood personalities, the stars of the stage or concert hall, represent a personal achievement strikingly different from the humanitarian heroes and heroines. Superstars are super because they have outperformed the competition in or on the field. This competitive excellence is not for the sake of the community

18. Martin Luther King, Jr., "Pilgrimage to Nonviolence," *The Christian Century*, LXXVII (13 April 1960) 440.

primarily, but for the sake of the individual's self-esteem. There is a secondary beneficiary of a team, organization, or nation, but this is not primary.

American Christianity has not escaped this individualism. The dream of being self-sufficient, of making it on one's own, of being apart from the majority is not a totally bad dream. It can be just as bad to romanticize human relationships in a way that denies autonomy. In that case, adult relationships are reduced to the therapeutic model, a model that is actually a subtle form of individualism.[19] Neither model contributes to a community of memory and the bonding that enables shared stories to be told.

Heroes and heroines are meant to engender respect for the values that are the core of communities of memory. Villains are sinister reminders that the community also has stories of evil to tell about itself. Christian communities of memory have gospels that embody a variety of symbolic and real heroines, heroes, and villains. Genuine communities of memory show their authenticity by the kinds of stories they tell. Any human community has stories of triumphs and of failures. Ideals are not easily grasped and consistently lived by any community. The genuine community does not fear telling stories of failure, for the whole story is greater than any one of the parts. As each communal generation learns the stories, the images of heroines and heroes will be created anew. Heroic images recount and reconstitute the past into the present and future.[20]

Christian communities, like all human communities, know of prophetic heroines and heroes. The images have meaning not only in context of a past but also in a present and future. Prophetic images indicate that prophets can stand within a community or apart from the community. In either case, the prophet can point to the need for the community to change only because God's pathos for the people lives through the heart of the prophet.[21]

Staying at the heart of the community is difficult for American Christians whom later history may judge to be prophetic. On the

19. Bellah, *Habits of the Heart* 284-89.
20. Alisdair MacIntyre, *After Virtue* (South Bend: University of Notre Dame Press, 1981) 30-33.
21. Walter Brueggeman, *The Prophetic Imagination* (Philadelphia: Fortress Press, 1978) 44-61, 109-13.

whole, Americans seem better at creating corporations and managing organizations than at dealing with long-term community commitments. "Communities are more complex and threatening to the American psyche."[22]

Christian vocation provides a certain corrective for the individualism and independence that characterize American heroism. The baptismal vocation is to authentic personhood within a community. Heroic self-actualization is not a competitive adventure, but one in which each acknowledges the unique graces and gifts of oneself and others for the task of mediating the kingdom.[23]

There is a certain restlessness about the American spirit that militates against confinement by any community. The status quo has always been a subject for potential change and even revolt. Americans are never quite satisfied with the present. A brief look at social history points to the variety of such dissatisfaction in the sporadic movements toward liberty and justice for all.[24] This restlessness can be a culturally friendly context for the Christian community of memory, for the call to conversion can be manifest in restlessness.

The counter-cultural movements of the sixties were results of a certain restlessness or dissatisfaction with the present. Three results of those movements can be mirrored in the present variety of movements in American religions.

First, the social movement that resulted in a renewed emphasis on power and wealth to preserve independence is a renewed form of individualism. There are churches whose members are comparably self-contained in the insular boundaries of a church, a source of power. Second, another movement attempted to alleviate insecurity in a rapidly changing society by returning to authoritarianism. Religion, politics, and other institutions cen-

22. Anthony T. Padovano, *America: Its People, Its Promise* (Cincinnati: St. Anthony Messenger Press, 1975) 25.
23. James W. Fowler, *Becoming Adult, Becoming Christian* (New York: Harper and Row, 1984) 84-105.
24. Nancy Cott and Elizabeth H. Pleck, ed., *A Heritage of Her Own* (New York: Simon and Schuster, 1979) 136-161, 182-221, 507-41; Martin Luther King, Jr., *Why We Can't Wait* (New York: 1964); Wendell Berry, *The Unsettling of America: Culture and Agriculture* (New York: Avon, 1977); Dorothy Day, *The Long Loneliness* (New York: 1952).

tralized more authority in a few. A third movement renewed the biblical vision of a global community in which the dignity of every person became an imperative.[25] For some churches this meant a critical appraisal of the powerless within as well as without the boundaries of the churches.

A new consciousness and interest in mysticism may lend support or opposition to any of the three movements. For many Americans mystical exerience can make formal communities both undesirable and unnecessary. Withdrawal into a purely private experience of God is a persistent temptation in any religion that separates the divine from the human. Christian mysticism, on the other hand, is authenticated by its incarnational expression and mediation through the community. Personal holiness or union with Jesus Christ is a union with the Body of Christ that is potentially all people.

The churches cannot ignore the religious individualism in the contemporary emphasis in American spirituality. Cultural memory affects the shape and credibility of the Christian memory, but it does not obscure the memory. The life given for all has a power that is created anew whenever Christians gather to enter into it. There is a conversion that is required for the Christian memory to remain alive. Today, that conversion may require the churches to:

> deepen and direct and discipline that inwardness in the light of faith until God leads us back to a vision of the public and to faithful action on the public's behalf.[26]

Many value judgments can be made about the good and bad aspects of the American community of memory. Whatever the judgments are, it remains true that the Christian memory lives within these cultural boundaries, though it is not determined by them. Early church leaders did not see a necessary incompatibility

25. Bellah, *Habits of the Heart* 349-52; The positions are developed at length by Marilyn Ferguson, *The Aquarian Conspiracy* (Boston: Houghton Mifflin, 1980) 361-403.
26. Parker J. Palmer, *Company of Strangers: Christians and the Renewal of America's Public Life* (New York: Crossroad, 1981) 155.

between the American dream and the Christian dream. Most saw a certain mutuality.

> The Church of America must be, of course, as Catholic as (the church) in Jerusalem or Rome; but as far as her garments assume colour from the local landscapes, she must be American.[27]

On one hand, it is a fact of history that the church can become an unconscious captive of the values, rituals, and power symbols of some particular culture or networks of culture. Theology is a human enterprise that functions within certain world views. The liturgical spirituality of the church can serve as a corrective to the necessarily partial theologies that order the life of the church. The Christian memory proclaims a kingdom dream. The orthodox celebration of this memory can mediate a discerning critique of the church and society that is a preliminary to conversion. The next section will consider some facets of the Christian dream and the American dream.

THE CHRISTIAN DREAM AND THE AMERICAN DREAM

The Christian dream and the early American dream have shared the ideals of liberty and justice for all, of a manifest destiny, and of heroism that has a price. Both dreams have challenges arising from the nature of the community that tries to make the dream come true. To effect such a transformation, a critical consciousness and a hopeful imagination for the possible are essential. There are at least four points of divergence as well as convergence of the American dream and the Christian dream.

Pilgrim Restlessness

A pilgrim restlessness characterizes many Americans. The mobility of Americans externally is one manifestation of the restless inner space that has been such a fascination for American psychologists. That restlessness can be an impetus to the holy rest-

---

27. This reflection by Archbishop John Ireland is quoted in William Sperry, *Religion in America* (New York: Macmillan, 1946) 219.

lessness that moves the people of God to transform this earth into a better mediator of the kingdom of God.

Though fascination with one's own center could be a manifestation of narcissism, it could also be a necessary journey to discover the kingdom that is within as well as without. No one can become communal until they are "centered," for a "union of centers" is the source of community in Christ. Changing moods and limits of the heart are a prayerful part of the Christian dream shared by the community of memory.

> God of power and Lord of mercy ... direct our steps in our everyday efforts. May the changing moods of the human heart and the limits which our failings impose on hope never blind us to you, source of all good. (Alternative Prayer, 31 Sunday in Ordinary Time)

There is a relationship of restlessness and dreams. When dreams have not been accomplished, when obvious failures accompany hopes, a community becomes restless. The church's year of grace incorporates some of this restlessness into the memory needed to direct and correct the sentiment. On civil holidays the church remembers what some may have forgotten.

> ... they fashioned a nation where all may live as one. Their message lives on in our midst as a task for us today and a promise for tomorrow. We thank you, Father, for your blessings in the past and for all that, with your help, we must yet achieve. (Preface 82)

Real Dreams Have Costs

The cry of Patrick Henry, "Give me liberty or give me death," is complemented by the Christian awareness that there cannot be one without the other. Liberty and justice for all, the willingness of the powerful to empower the less powerful, is not easily accomplished. The cross of Christ is always in danger of being spiritualized. When that happens, the "next life" becomes a future antidote for passive endurance of the injustices of this life.

The cross of Christ proclaims the danger that accompanies those who make "this life" a partial realization of "next life." Salva-

151

tion cannot be passively spiritualized into a future as long as the dangerous memory of the cross keeps the community alive.

> The Father of mercies has given us an example of unselfish love in the sufferings of his only Son. Through your service of God and neighbor, may you receive his countless blessings . . . He humbled himself for our sakes. May you follow his example and share in his resurrection. (Solemn Blessing, Palm Sunday)

The memory of the cross proclaims that the victim of violence is often the one who is least violent. There is a cost to "unselfish love." The Kennedys, Martin Luther King, Jr., Archbishop Oscar Romero, Ita Ford, Jean Donovan, Dorothy Kazell, Maura Clarke, and a host of less publicized persons ended life in a violent manner. Today in South America the victim status that results from attempts at social transformation affects many people whose lives will never be publicized as heroic adventures. A Guatemalan Indian describes one of the scenes of violence against a catechist and his small community.

> They crucified them alive in the middle of the road, two stakes through the hands, one through the naked stomach, another through the bare feet, and one through the head.[28]

The authenticity of the Christian memory is tested at the foot of the cross. Apostolic succession is primarily determined here as the tradition is passed on. To break bread is to engage in communal transformation of the world. Crucifixion takes a variety of forms in the church and in the world that become clearer as the community remembers who it is called to be. A day of Thanksgiving reflects the ideals of both the American memory and the Christian memory.

> Once you chose a people and gave them a destiny, and when you brought them out of bondage to freedom, they carried with them

28. This quote is a personal testimony awaiting publication. It appears in Juan Hernandez Pico, "Martyrdom Today in Latin America: Stumbling-block, Folly and Power of God," Concilium 163, *Martyrdom Today,* ed. Johannes-Baptist Metz and Edward Schillebeeckx (New York: Seabury, 1983).

the promise that all could be blessed, that all could be free . . . It happens to us still in our time. (Preface 84, Thanksgiving Day)

The reality of that ideal, in the contours of particular times and places of history, may be less clear. In theory the orthodox memory of the Christian community calls forth a critical voice for dignity in any cultural or ecclesial silencing of freedom. There are always prophets who will try to raise the critical consciousness of cultural and ecclesial communities.

Brothers, you are from your own people. You are killing your own brother campesinos . . . It is high time you recovered your conscience . . . In the name of God, yes, and in the name of this suffering people whose groans rise to heaven more loudly every day, I beg you, I ask you, I order you in the name of God—stop the repression![29]

Neither the American dream nor the Christian dream can be spiritualized if either is to come true. Revolution may be necessary to effect life, liberty, and dignity for all people. But the revolution will begin with a conversion within, so that eventual reconciliation can overthrow the violence without. That inner conversion can not be merely privatized holiness, for the community is at the heart of the process.

Privatized Holiness

Private spaces need protection in the American psyche. Some degree of spatial separation seems imperative to communal formation. The spatial separation, exterior or interior, can be symbolized through some of the heroic images that are found in the history of literature. The social psyche and the need for spatial separation from the community were symbolized by the lone cowboy, like Shane, who rides off into the sunset as a restless hero leaving crying women behind.

The psychic separation manifest in American individualism, self-containment, and the desire to journey alone are also present

29. M. Sobrino and Cardenal Maro, *La voz de los sin voz, La palabra viva de Monsenor Romero* (San Salvador: UCA, 1980) 291.

in spatial constructions. Having separate spaces even in physical togetherness is a necessity. Architects introduced doors and walls to mark off and preserve private spaces in homes. Churches had restricted spaces and common spaces to symbolize another kind of order, an order divided by a "communion" rail. Prayer stalls in churches and monasteries separated persons from inadvertently touching. Airlines keep middle seats empty when possible for reasons of psychic space as much as physical space. Americans appreciate and seem to need the distance.

In a history that accents utilitarian individualism with the concomitant desire for privacy, the Christian memory can be a necessary reminder of community. In the Christian dream the life given "for you" presumes an identification with "all." The compassion of Christ that is the living memory may be best expressed today through the face of justice for all.[30]

Through the gospel and the eucharist . . . make us a sign of your love for all people, and help us to show forth the living presence of Christ in the world. (Prayer for the Local Church, E)

Christ is a clear model of the universality of compassion which the community remembers. Christ has come to "lift up all things to himself," and to "restore the unity to creation." (Preface 4, Christmas II) "The suffering and death of your Son brought life to the whole world, moving our hearts to praise your glory." (Preface 17, Passion of the Lord I) "In Christ, a new age has dawned, the long reign of sin is ended, a broken world has been renewed." (Preface 24, Easter IV) "Open our eyes to see your hand at work in the beauty of creation, in the splendor of human life. Touched by your hand, our world is holy." (Prayer of 17 Sunday in Ordinary Time)

In an American privacy mentality, celebrating the covenant memory may be a challenging experience. Life direction toward the communal has costs. "Show us how great is the call to serve, that we may share in the peace of Christ who offered his life in the service of all." (Prayer of 24 Sunday in Ordinary Time)

The renewed awareness of the biblical call to universal concern

30. Francis X. Meehan, *A Contemporary Social Spirituality* (Maryknoll: Orbis Books, 1982) 1-24, 28-33.

and action for the dignity of every person provides a culturally friendly climate for the Christian memory. The variety of liberation movements toward mutuality and away from racism, sexism, and ethnicism can serve as a corrective for future visions and dreams. The new creation has not been accomplished. But movements can pinpoint clear areas where the non-universality of the new creation is evident.

American cultural memory points to the opposition of the new creation as well as to the formation of it. Christian churches opposed the social movements for abolition of slavery, for women's and blacks' rights to vote, and so on. Sacralization of an older creation prevented the churches from being part of the newer movements of liberty and justice for all.[31]

To "do this in memory of me" is to enter into the danger of the creation. Some things legitimately die as Christians renew the meaning of the memory and hand on the tradition. If these remnants do not die, there will be fewer Christians who are willing to receive what is being handed on. To proclaim the death of the Lord until he comes is a call to continue in the formation of a new creation in Christ.

The contours of that new creation may be as surprising as the imagination of God revealed in and through the mystery of Jesus Christ. The critical consciousness heightened by entering into the memory of the death and resurrection will necessitate new structures to mediate the memory. The hopeful part of the dream is that the critical questions are being raised today.

> What kind of church will it be in which the pastoral care and anointing of the sick, the witnessing and blessing of Christian marriages, the reconciliation of sinners, the celebration of the Eucharist, and the formation of new Christians are recognized as the right and responsibility of the baptized? What corrections and revisions in self-understanding will be demanded of the laity, of presbyters and deacons, of bishops, of the bishop of Rome as these . . . seek to open themselves to the value and truth of new

31. H. Shelton Smith, Robert T. Handy, and Lefferts A. Loetscher, *American Christianity*, vol. 2 (New York: Scribner's Sons, 1963) 167-212; 407-16; Rosemary Radford Reuther, "Home and Work: Women's Roles and the Transformation of Values," in *Woman: New Dimensions*, ed. Walter Burghardt (New York: Paulist Press, 1977) 71-83.

possibility in the liturgical celebration of the mystery of Christ at work in the world?[32]

Liturgical spirituality heightens the consciousness that critically discerns how the cross and resurrection are mediated in the world today. The living memory, Jesus Christ, leads the community into that future where the kingdom dream shall be known as it cannot be known now. The liturgy reminds the community of memory that they need not fear any future shape the memory may take. Christ "is still our priest, our advocate who always pleads our cause." (Preface 23, Easter III) Christ "has passed beyond our sight, not to abandon us but to be our hope . . . Where he has gone, we hope to follow." (Preface 26, Ascension I)

SUMMARY

Christians are a community of memory within many different cultural communities of memory. Like other communities of memory, Christians remember the dreams of the past as a basis for creating the future. Like other communities of memory, there may be times when the community forgets, and becomes imprisoned by restraints of the culture or by the sacralized restraints of the faith community.

The American community of memory was forged from an ideal that was a Christian ideal as well. To have life, liberty, and dignity, required some sacrifice of individual preferences for the good of the community. Only a community could protect the individual rights. Communities could survive only to the extent there were self-sacrificing individuals who kept the memory alive.

Biblical churches grew up in America alongside utilitarian individualism. Each affected the other. Biblical piety acquired shades of individualism. But individualism also reflected some communal concerns through heroic figures. The countercultural movements of the sixties provided basic developmental currents that continue to be reflected in social and ecclesial circles. What the future holds will be influenced by the sustained strength of

32. Mary Collins, "Obstacles to Liturgical Creativity," Concilium 162, *Liturgy: A Creative Tradition*, ed. Mary Collins and David Power (New York: Seabury, 1983) 24.

these currents, as well as by an orthodox renewal of the Christian memory.

The cross and resurrection provide contours of a dangerous memory that serves as a critique of movements in every age. Power that brings independence to some at the cost of oppression to others has no place either in the American dream or in the Christian dream. Authoritarianism that confuses unity with choiceless conformity is foreign to both dreams.

There is a universality that is essential to the formation of the Christian dream. The lack of universality today may be critiqued best by those who feel they are not or cannot be part of the present limitations of the dream. The dream will never be fully accomplished, but that is why dreams exist that are larger than a measurable lifetime.

If the Christian memory is to have a vital impact on the shape of the world to come, the liturgical life of the church will require ongoing renewal. The place to begin with that renewal was a more universal reform such as Vatican II began. But today the renewal may need to continue and assume shape through the particular communities that celebrate the Christian memory. The intimate has always been a legitimate mediator of the infinite. The final chapter will point to some of these aspects of the future of the memory.

Further Thematic Development

1. The universality of the Christian memory must be mediated through the particularity of cultures. What might this mean liturgically for the spiritualities of the Orient, Africa, India, Latin America, and newly emerging cultures?

SOME SOURCES

Cuttat, J. "Christian Experience and Oriental Spirituality," Concilium 49, *Secularization and Spirituality*, ed. C. Duquoc (New York: Paulist, 1969) 131-42.

Dwyer, W. "The Theologian in the Ashram," Concilium 115, *Doing Theology in New Places*, ed. J. Jossua and J. B. Metz (New York: Seabury, 1979) 92-101.

Elizondo, V., and N. Greinacher, ed. Concilium 144, *Tensions Be-*

tween the Churches of the First World and the Third World (New York: Seabury, 1981).

Geffré, C., ed. Concilium 151, *The Church and Racism* (New York: Seabury, 1982).

Geffré, C. and B. Luneau, ed. Concilium 106, *The Churches of Africa: Future Prospects* (New York: Seabury, 1977).

Geffré, C. and J. Spae, ed. Concilium 126, *China as a Challenge to the Church* (New York: Seabury, 1979).

Griffiths, B. *Christ in India* (New York: Scribners, 1966).

Gutierrez, G. *We Drink From Our Own Wells* (New York: Orbis, 1983).

Ngindu, Mushete. "The Church of Christendom in the Face of New Cultures," Concilium 146, *Where Does the Church Stand?*, ed. G. Alberigo and G. Gutierrez (New York: Seabury, 1981) 53-6.

Pannikar, R. *The Unknown Christ of Hinduism* (London: Darton, Longman and Todd, 1981).

2. The relationship of local churches and basic communites to the universal church raises a number of issues about the nature of a Christian church. What are some of these issues that are being considered today?

SOME SOURCES

Pro Mundi Vita, #80, *Parishes Without Priests*, 1979.

Pro Mundi Vita, #81, *Basic Communities in the Church*, 1980.

Boff, Clodovis, "The Nature of Basic Christian Communities," Concilium 144, *Tensions Between the Churches*, ed. V. Elizondo and N. Greinacher 53-58.

Feret, H. "The Word of God and Its Sovereignty in Today's Church," Concilium 146, *Where Does the Church Stand?*, ed. G. Alberigo and G. Gutierrez 3-13.

McBrien, R. "The Underground Church in the United States," Concilium 49, *Secularization and Spirituality*, ed. C. Duquoc (New York: Paulist Press, 1969) 109-20.

Rahner, K. *Concern for the Church* (New York: Crossroad, 1981) 103-14.

Rahner, K. *The Shape of the Church to Come* (New York: Seabury, 1975) 29-44, 108-22.

van Nieuwenhove, J. "Implications of Puebla for the Whole Church," Concilium 144, pp. 65-69.

Whitehead, Evelyn and James. *Community of Faith* (New York: Seabury, 1982).

3. The North American experience has provided a setting of early idealism, dreams, and eventual illusions. Freedom and justice for all, unity, community, are values that have existed side by side with practices of racism, sexism, individualism, and fundamentalism. Choose any one of the themes and briefly develop the paradox of ideals and practices within American churches and spiritualities. From the tapestry constructed as a whole, critique the adequacy or inadequacy of liturgical revisions of texts for civil holidays, sanctoral calendar and accompanying texts (especially noting the Commons).

SOME SOURCES

Bellah, R., and others, ed. *Habits of the Heart* (Los Angeles: University of Berkeley, 1985).

Bellah, R., and C. Glock, ed. *The New Religious Consciousness* (Los Angeles: University of California, 1976).

Kennedy, Eugene. *The Now and Future Church* (New York: Doubleday, 1984).

Mead, Sidney. *The Fire We Can Light* (New York: Doubleday, 1973).

Mead, Sidney. *The Nation with the Soul of a Church* (New York: Harper and Row, 1975) 1-77.

Oden, Thomas. *The Intensive Group Experience: The New Pietism* (Philadelphia: Westminster, 1972).

Padovano, Anthony. *America: Its People, Its Promise* (Cincinnati: St. Anthony Messenger Press, 1975).

Philibert, P. "Dissent and Protest in the American Church," Concilium 78, *Contestation in the Church,* ed. T. Urresti (New York: Herder, 1971) 32-39.

Reuther, Rosemary, and Rosemary S. Keller, ed. *Women and Religion in America* (New York: Harper and Row, 1981-), vols. 1, 2.

Smith, H. Shelton, Robert T. Handy, and Lefferts A. Loetscher. *American Christianity* (New York: Scribner's, 1963), vol. 1, 11.

Trisco, R. "Democratic Influence on the Election of Bishops and Pastors and on the Administration of Dioceses and Parishes in the U.S.A.," Concilium 77, *Election and Consensus in the Church,* ed. G. Alberigo and A. Weiler (New York: Herder, 1972) 132-38.

EIGHT

A FUTURE MEMORY:
NEW HEAVEN AND NEW EARTH

Behold, I make all things new
(Rv 21:5)

WHEN THE APOCALYPTIC SEER WROTE OF A "NEW HEAVEN AND A NEW earth," the initiative of God was clear. "Behold, I make all things new!" (Rv 21:1,5) Liturgical memory includes this vision of the future when God "will wipe every tear from their eyes." (Rv 21:3,4) Christian liturgy is a focused testament to that ultimate liturgy in which all shall be made new.

But the future of the memory is not an alternative world to that known in the present. Believers who gather until the Lord comes in glory know that the unfolding drama of human history is the context for epiphanies of the Lord. Because of the incarnation, death, and resurrection, everything somehow belongs to the Lord. "In this liturgy of the world, all biographies—human and divine— meet, clash, and are finally reconciled."[1]

Liturgical spirituality emerges from the living memory that Emmanuel necessarily works through imperfect people and through a groaning creation. Believers drawn toward the future of the memory know that worship does more than rehearse and order what is already experienced and old about the present. The testimony to the orthodoxy of remembering is to work toward that

1. Nathan Mitchell, "The Spirituality of Christian Worship," *Spirituality Today* 34:1 (Spring 1982) 10.

new heaven and new earth that is the Christian kingdom. If humans do not wipe tears from each other's eyes, the Lord will have a difficult task of renewing the earth.

The new heaven and the new earth may seem to be a distant and invisible hope. But like all hope, the hope for the new heaven and the new earth requires envisioning structures that can best mediate the dream. That raises the issue of religious imagination in general and American religious imagination in particular. American history points to an imagination of futures that differed from that of Europeans. The American dream of a new earth was imagined and mediated through Christian symbols.

This chapter will briefly summarize some characteristics of "newness" in the religious imagination of the American people, symbolized through the pioneer spirit. Second, the themes of dream and apocalyptic will be contextualized within the Christian notion of apocalyptic. Third, some observations on possible futures for the liturgical memory and domestic spirituality will conclude the chapter.

RELIGIOUS IMAGINATION: PIONEERS OF THE NEW EARTH

In 1854 an ecclesial historian named Philip Schaff was the chosen scholar to lecture German churchmen about American religious experience. Though there was some degree of continuity between European and American religious imagination, Schaff had already come to the conclusion that America's religious imagination was in fact quite different. America seemed:

> ... destined to be the Phoenix grave ... of all European churches and sects, of Protestantism and Romanism. Something wholly new will gradually arise. Organizing energies are already present, and the Spirit of God broods over them ... to call forth from the chaos a beautiful creation.[2]

2. Philip Schaff, "America: A Sketch of the Political, Social, and Religious Character of the United States of North America." Two lectures were delivered under this title before the German Diet at Frankfurt-am-Main, Berlin, September, 1864. The lectures were printed without pagination in 1865. (New York: Scribner, 1865).

Other American watchers agreed that something new was at work in the American experience. First, traditionally antagonistic European ethnic groups had to learn to live in harmony in the new land. When the Constitutional Convention met in 1787, religious freedom was pronounced without any religious group officially clamoring for it. Religious freedom marked "one of the two most profound revolutions in the history of the church."[3] Why? Because national churches were essential for national unity.

> It was a universal assumption that the stability of the social order and the safety of the state demanded the religious solidarity of all the people in one church. Every responsible thinker . . . held to this as an axiom.[4]

It was "a great experiment" to allow a new experience of religious freedom to emerge as part of an American dream of liberty. Jefferson rightly believed that the great experiment was compatible with the ideals of rationalists and pietists, two influential groups in the emerging nation. Both groups believed that the integral individual was free only in context of the larger community. It was the community that had to protect as well as confirm personal freedom and its limits.

> We have experienced the quiet as well as the comfort which results from leaving everyone to profess freely and openly those principles of religion which are inductions of his own reason, and the serious convictions of his own inquiries.[5]

The American community could not share a common past, because there was no common past. There was only a shared sense of the newness of the present, and the dream of a future that

3. John Wesley, *Sermons on Several Occasions* (New York: Lane and Tippett, 1851), vol. 2, 392.
4. Winifred E. Garrison, "Characteristics of American Organized Religion," *Annals of the American Academy of Political and Social Science* CCLVI (March 1948) esp. 17-20.
5. Thomas Jefferson, *The Complete Jefferson Containing His Major Writings, Published and Unpublished, Except His Letters,* ed. Saul K. Padover (New York: Duell, Sloan, and Pearce, 1943) 676.

was lived out in the present. Christianity provided symbols for interpreting the experience of the land being like a new heaven and a new earth. The covenant image assured the people that God was with them to whatever extent they furthered the rights of all, particularly the powerless who had little voice.

The community was the bearer of God's wisdom. This wisdom was known through conflict of opinion, since each opinion was a partial perspective on truth. Dissent was essential to the American imagination. Errors "cease to be dangerous when it is permitted to freely contradict them."[6]

The vastness of space called forth various symbolic types of explorers or pioneers. Each suggests corollaries of religious imagination, freedom, and response to a social gospel popularized through the efforts of Walter Rauschenbusch.[7] The symbolic types of pioneers can be called the hearty explorers, the reluctant pioneers, and the settling pioneers. Each can be described as follows.

The hearty explorers are symbolized by the type of pioneer who continued westward, challenged by the unexplored, invigorated by the unknown and by what could be. These pioneers lived with little nostalgia for what was left behind. Their Lord was a Lord of the future who would assuredly meet them there if they did not lose heart. As they moved forward, the patterns of the old could not and ought not constrict the creative patterns that were necessary in the new land of dignity and liberty for all. As the social gospel was popularized in the nineteenth century, this group took an active part in social reforms, sharing power through structures of education, politics, and self-help. The new patterns of equality for all races and ethnic groups, and for women as well, emerged from their religious imagination of the new heaven and new earth they were called to form.

The reluctant pioneers have dragging feet that are only circumstantially directed into the future. They have never really left

6. Jefferson, "Notes on Religion, October, 1776," in Padover, *The Complete Jefferson* 947.
7. Walter Rauschenbusch, *Christianizing the Social Order* (New York: Macmillan, 1912). Sidney Mead names and characterizes the symbolic pioneer types in *The Lively Experiment* (New York: Harper and Row, 1963).

the structures, sentiments, or contents of the memories of home behind them. Their Lord is a Lord who wipes away every lonely tear, and who refreshes them to endure the exile of the present. Passionate memories of a secure past shape the image of heaven that the revivalist hymns capture so well. The reluctant pioneers feel that freedom exists to stabilize the new by structuring it into known patterns of the old. There is a paralyzing fear of the new spaces, of what could be, when no older structure can contain the vision. If the Lord is changeless, then everything must have a clearly defined place that humans may not change. Class distinctions, gender roles, roles in the churches are set by God and not to be altered in any so-called new society. For these pioneers God does not intend equality but ordering of relationships. This group opposed the ending of slavery as well as the voting rights of black men and all women.

The settling pioneers are those who moved once, and decided to settle in a particular space. They brought what was useful of the old world to order the space of the new world, namely, art, architecture, familial and social patterns. These settlers are the true conservatives of the past, as well as the builders for the future. They can discard the old structures when these no longer facilitate life in the new world. Their Lord calls them to work hard for the new heaven and the new earth, shaping the kingdom through their efforts in tune with the Lord. They know that freedom, liberty for all, and justice can only work when there are carefully balanced structures to confirm and order the expression of values of individuals and communities. Their Christian source of continuity is the Spirit, not the past structures that mediated the Spirit. Thus, these are capable of letting go of the old when the Lord seems to be doing something new.

What can be concluded from the symbolic types of pioneers? First, there is a cultural conditioning of the American religious imagination that affects every believer in some way. Second, while entire church communities may doctrinally reflect a particular symbolic pioneer imagination, there are individuals of the three symbolic types in every community. Third, in this age of more ecumenical liturgical prayer, the people with similar religious imagination across the churches may pray with more of a sense of common unity than those of the same church.

Today the religious imagination of Americans is affected by a "religious awakening." In American religious history a major religious awakening results from some resolution of social turmoil. The turmoil is marked by communal loss of faith in institutions, authority, values, and dreams. In the process of awakening, it is the "common people" rather than the leaders, institutions, or authorities, who define new dreams and visions. In the process of religious awakening the people pass from an inadequate world view to a new and more comprehensive one.

There is an ability to identify some trends of this current ideological shift that is affecting, and will continue to do so, American religious imagination.[8] Different American watchers agree that the world view that is now emerging will include at least the following pieces. Some form of Judaeo-Christian socialism will be foundational to the new political ideology. A new dream will be created from an earlier national dream. This dream will include the hope for world community, with the national self-sacrifice necessary to accomplish that hope. A sense of limits will characterize the use of resources locally and globally. The vision of a life-giving and empathetic God, or Divine Power, will integrate the world view stressing mutuality and dignity of women and men, of racial and ethnic groups, of old and young. Success will not be measured as much by economic status and power as by the quality of human relationships. "The awakening is moving and changing American life," but it will take another generation or more for "it must escape the enculturation of old ways."[9]

When the old ways begin to disintegrate, and no direction immediately appears for the present, the literary form of apocalyptic becomes popular. The kinds of apocalyptic and the reflections of the American spirit mediated through apocalyptic are an interesting commentary on American religious imagination.

8. William G. McLoughlin, *Revivals, Awakenings, and Reform* (Chicago: University of Chicago, 1978) 1-22.
9. McLoughlin, *Revivals* 216. Similar approaches are found in Anthony C. Wallace, "Revitalization Movements," *American Anthropology* 58 (1956) 264-81; Cushing Stout, *The New Heavens and the New Earth* (New York: Harper and Row, 1974); Rufus E. Miles, Jr. *Awakening From the American Dream* (New York: Universe, 1976); Robert Bellah, *The Broken Covenant* (New York: Seabury, 1975).

APOCALYPTIC AND THE AMERICAN SPIRIT

The ideals of the early American dream were both formative and expressive of the first Americans. But human dreams give way to the realization that there are illusions, broken covenants, and shattered hopes. At these points the symbol of apocalyptic appears to reshape the dreams, or else to destroy the illusion of dreams. Apocalyptic works abound when the known world seems to be lost or disappearing, and no fixed new world seems to be appearing on the horizon. Existence itself is at stake.

Common to all true apocalyptic is a situation characterized by anomie, a loss of "world" or erosion of structures, psychic and cultural, with the consequent nakedness to Being or intermediary to the Mystery.[10]

American apocalyptic, like biblical apocalyptic, uses the three symbolic elements of catastrophe, judgment, and renewal. There is a failure in righteousness when any community simply gives up in the face of catastrophe. Righteousness shall only come when there is a willingness to continue building the new heaven and the new earth. The maturity of the call to conversion is apparent when naive optimism is rejected, and cynical inertia is overcome.

Christian apocalyptic provides some correctives for American literary apocalyptic. Christian apocalyptic claims that God in Christ is faithful and true to his promise. Literary apocalyptic is not so clear, at least in some forms of apocalyptic conclusions. There are varying interpretations of the contemporary cultural climate in the apocalyptic works of the twentieth century. Once the darkness of the human heart is recognized, and the masquerade of deceptions is clarified, humorous apocalyptic announces that all is not yet lost. Humorous apocalyptic works, characteristic of the seventies and eighties, recreate the human hopefulness that believes human transcendence is stronger than human weakness.

Contemporary apocalyptic literature, even if it provides a

10. Amos Wilder, "The Rhetoric of Ancient and Modern Apocalyptic," a paper presented to the American Academy of Religion, 1970, pp. 4-5 (xeroxed copy).

bridge to the future, does not sketch the dimensions of that future. The Christian language of hope provides a surer passage. Rebirth of meanings for the people can only come through those who are assured that something lies ahead.

> Apocalypse does not hold a carrot of eternity before believers . . . it stirs them to accept the agony of history as birth pangs of a new creation that they are part of.[11]

Christian apocalyptic is interested in the future as the solution to the past and present. Conversion through rebirth of the Christian dream within the ideals of the American dream is not impossible. John Courtney Murray focused one possibility when he advocated faith in "the people."

> The concept of "the people" is the crucial one in this present day, as it was in the past age that saw the birth of the institution of the state-church, which was itself based on a particular concept of "the people" . . . a work of discernment needs to be done on the tradition . . . in the face of the changing realities of the political order.[12]

In Christian liturgical tradition the people or the Body of Christ are the locus of the new heavens and the new earth. The American dream and the Christian dream have imaged varieties of possibilities for the new heaven and the new earth. Christian apocalyptic reveals that the dream shall be fulfilled. American apocalyptic hopes that the space of the future will not remain empty.

The present period of religious awakening suggests the need for transforming this earth into a better resemblance of the new

---

11. A comprehensive study of apocalyptic and its meanings in American literature has been done by John May, S.J., *Toward a New Earth: Apocalypse in the American Novel* (Notre Dame: University of Notre Dame, 1972) 213. See his summary and interpretation noted on pp. 1-41 and pp. 202-9.

12. John Courtney Murray, "The Problem of State Religion," *Theological Studies* XII:2 (June 1951) 163-64. Murray's entire article, pp. 160-67, provides an American foundation for his own contribution to the work of Vatican II on religious freedom.

earth of the kingdom. A starting point for this task is a greater in-digenization of liturgical life. There can be no vital universal church unless there are vital local churches. "But these local churches will be truly local only if they have their own distinctive culture and traditions."[13]

Distinctive culture and tradition can be difficult to trace. In the North American experience the vision of the past and present is just beginning to include racial, gender, and ethnic experiences that were traditionally missing pieces of the American dream. In the larger context of Christian universality, the liturgical life of the church reflects an extrinsic similarity of ritual that is only begin-ning to admit legitimate diversity.

Could the liturgical memory celebrated in the American im-agination mediate the Christian dream more effectively? What would be the starting point for such a process of "indigenization"? Are there communities of intimacy that have been overlooked in liturgical renewal of a more universal scope?

Liturgical memory has a future yet to come, for this is the new-ness that gives meaning to the Christian sense of time. But that fu-ture will be formed to the extent that kingdom dreams are incar-nationalized in particular times and places. The research already done on parish communities is one starting point for giving shape to the dream.[14] Another starting point is that with which this book shall conclude, the Christian family.

THE FAMILY: MEDIATOR OF THE CHRISTIAN MEMORY

Vatican II and subsequent documents have encouraged the concept of the family as a communal source of faith. But there has not been as much supportive reflection on domestic spirituality as there has been on clerical spirituality, lay spirituality, and minis-terial spirituality. There is a beginning of reflection that attempts

13. R. Kevin Seasoltz, *New Liturgy, New Laws* (Collegeville: The Liturgi-cal Press, 1980) 188. See pp. 182-211 for pastoral applications of this principle.
14. *The Parish in Transition,* ed. David Byers (Washington, D.C.: National Conference of Catholic Bishops, 1986); *Families; Black and Catholic, Catholic and Black* (Washington, D.C.: National Conference of Catholic Bishops, 1985).

to link family life to the liturgical life of the church. Future possibilities for liturgical life centered within the foundations of family life are not so clearly stated.[15]

The liturgical memory will be domesticated in some way in the future. Relational communities provide one form of domestication, a form already discussed earlier in this work. If futurists like Toffler and Naisbett are correct, "home" is no longer "place" but "relationships" that replace high tech with real or symbolic high touch. American concern over the changing nature of the family suggests that this relational grouping could well be the focus for liturgical indigenization.

> When signs of the times indicate that a country wishes to preserve
> its family and national traditions, or return to them, the Church will
> do well to follow in the same train or else face the embarrassment
> of an overstaying alien.[16]

American liturgists are aware that Christians are committed to an essential and universal unity in Christ. But once committed to that dimension of liturgical memory, there is a pragmatic awareness that there must be an ecclesial indigenization "not only in so-called missionary countries but also in places where the church has long been established."[17]

For the North American church such acculturation is very slow in coming. For years liturgists have observed that the values, history, images, and dreams inherent in a particular culture must enrich the euchological texts. For example, the dynamism of the ICEL translation of the Leonine Collect of Christmas reflects the active contemplation of an American culture, in contrast to the more classical contemplative admiration of the Roman response.[18]

---

15. *Family Ministry,* ed. Gloria Durka and Joanmarie Smith (Minneapolis: Winston, 1980) presents a good introduction to the concept of family as normative locus of liturgical life, pp. 182-200.
16. Anscar Chupungco, *Towards a Filipino Liturgy* (Manila: Benedictine Abbey, 1976) 47, cited in Seasoltz, *New Liturgy, New Laws* 187.
17. R. Kevin Seasoltz, "Cultural Pluralism and the Church's Prayer," *Liturgy* 3:2 (Spring 1983) 49.
18. Anscar Chupungco, "The Sacred Liturgy: The Unfinished Task," in *Remembering the Future,* ed. Carl Last (New York: Paulist Press, 1983) 87.

Universality is conscientiously preserved in official texts. But the possibility of incorporating the particular into the universal has procedures that indicate "the people" are not capable of praying with any legitimate creativity. A culturally removed body decides upon the appropriateness.[19] This leaves particularity to the homilist's reflections or to the private interpretations of the community.

Over a decade ago, Walter Burghardt observed that liturgists must critically filter a basically European tradition of prayer through American hearts and vision. Liturgy and theology is done in a whole world of ideas. An American critique of non-American theologians and liturgists means much more than just translating world theologians into the English language. It means participation of the community. "For a creative American worship, liturgical theologian, church musician, and worshiping community must learn to collaborate, to listen."[20]

There must be an appropriation of the cultural matrix out of which particular communities operate. This more specific suggestion acknowledges the cultural, ethnic, vocational, chronological, and gender specific matrix out of which particular communities pray. The young point out the need for the liturgy of the church to have greater pluralism, relationship to life, and some kind of human bonding of community that can be celebrated.[21] Though so-called "children's liturgies" may meet one segment of the Christian particularity of chronology, comparable concern has not yet found its way into ritual reforms comprehending the aged. The ethnic and gender specific communities are only beginning to come into focus, but under a "paraliturgical" umbrella. Familial communities have not received much support for liturgical prayer in the homes.

There is a dangerous novelty about the kingdom of God that can make it "theologically sound to celebrate the mystery of salva-

19. This issue is discussed further by Gordon Truitt, "Liturgy as a School of Prayer: A Question," *Spiritual Life* 27:1 (Spring 1981) pp. 3-13.
20. Walter Burghardt, S.J., "A Theologian's Challenge to Liturgy," *Theological Studies* 35:2 (June 1974) 248.
21. José Aldazabal, "The Liturgy Should Learn from the Young," Concilium 162, *Liturgy: A Creative Tradition,* ed. Mary Collins and David Power (New York: Seabury, 1983) 86-92.

tion using forms which assert the dawning reign of God in human history in all its particularity."[22] Liturgical assemblies symbolically manifest the tension between human achievement and the reign of God. Corrections and revisions of self-understanding will have to occur among the laity and the ordained ministers if institutional churches and their liturgical assemblies are to be creative of the Christian dream in American surroundings.

The Christian tradition in its early life provided the household model as a vital center that allowed for a diversity of Christian activities. This included instructions, baptizing, social networking, and, of course, eucharistic celebration. Even in the early stages of Christianity, when temple and synagogue were larger contexts for prayer, the gathered household community was maintained as a viable symbol of the new creation in Christ. Here, the gatherings of thirty to forty Christians were not dictated by cultural conventions. The household churches had a unity that was counter-cultural to the separations and distinctions of the social milieu. Unity, authority for mutuality, and service of and for all were the loci of the gathered community.

There were networks of these churches that respected the plurality of experiences of the paschal mystery mediated through ethnic particularities, social classes, and other variations in life experiences. This did not distract from the universality of the Body of Christ. The new creation in Christ was large enough for a legitimate diversity of experience and expression of prayer that was affirmed through mission.[23]

Clearly, today is a different century and a different cultural milieu. However, the centrality of the family as a symbol of the church gathered in love and unity remains true. An extension includes the relational prayer communities that often react to an impersonal corporate symbol of church. Some fifteen years of experience with the base communities of Latin America have shown the possibilities such communities have for reform. If people share a similar dream, they also share a similar power and energy for the shaping of the future.

22. Mary Collins, "Obstacles to Liturgical Creativity," Concilium 162, *Liturgy: A Creative Tradition,* ed. Mary Collins and David Power 23.
23. John H. Elliott, "Philemon and House Churches," *The Bible Today* 22:3 (May 1984) 145-50.

This means much structural reshaping of accountability, collaboration, eucharistic presidency, and new outlines of laity and priesthood. In the Latin American church the collaboration required has brought new vitality to the church, and new questions about an outmoded seminary system. Lay leadership is, officially, not yet "sacramental," but the acknowledgement of that reality cannot be far away.[24]

A Latin American cultural and ecclesial-political setting suggesting a house church cannot be transplanted to North America. But the analogous emphasis on house church can embrace the Christian dream and its gracious corollaries in the American dream. A house church, the family, suggests a locus for liturgical prayer that liturgists may wish to consider seriously.

An American contribution to the particularity and universality of the Body of Christ could be the clear construction of a liturgical prayer compendium to be used in the domestic church. A group with composite expertise in liturgical symbols, meanings, traditions, poetic expression, aesthetic sensitivities, and experience of the time tensions in family life, could be gathered to work on simple home celebrations related to the liturgical year. The compendium might include ecclesial, civil, and familial celebrations within the environment of liturgical memory. The natural ritualizing potential of children would be taken into account, as well as the variety of groupings.

Table prayer related to the liturgical year, simple morning and evening prayer suitable for different chronological groups, and memorial celebrations around the table could be included. The civil year of potential grace and the ecclesial year of grace could dialogue more effectively if the awakening is to bear fruit. In all cases, a sensitizing of parental leaders of the domestic gatherings could facilitate a legitimate creativity that is appropriate within some gatherings, but not applicable to all other such gatherings.

The domestic church in North America will never assume the same potential for ecclesial renewal that it already has in Europe, Latin America, or other countries. The American dream has different shapes than other dreams. Dreams shape familial life, as well as ecclesial and cultural life. Liturgical memory will embrace

24. Edward Cleary, O. P., *Crisis and Change* (New York: Orbis, 1985) esp. 125-45.

these dreams if there is a participative possibility for the American "bearer of wisdom," the people.

There is future to be shaped in every age through the memory celebrated with bread and wine. A more conscious focus upon the domestic church, the theological and liturgical possibilities of its position at the heart of human experience, suggests this is one way to revitalize the dream. This dream "comes in the form of an invitation to reach into the here and now and bring forth God's own desired future," a future in which Christ will make all things new.[25]

SUMMARY

The American spirit has a history of expression that is still in process of being lived and written. The American dream, originally similar to a Christian dream of dignity and liberty for all people, assumed new expressions in a land whose people had no common past. Early in American history, the peoples who had been antagonistic in other lands had to learn to live in peace and unity in the new land.

American religionists were aware of the newness of the religious imagination of the people. A new potential for peace and union of religious groups was facilitated by separation of church from state. All people could practice the religion to which they felt called. The radical shift from a long term philosophical assumption, that order in a land could exist only if government and church were one, was incomprehensible to Europeans.

It was not so incomprehensible to a people whose diversity was a source of wisdom rather than antipathy. The people became the bearers of wisdom through unity, conflict, dissent, and the forum to discuss differences openly. This American way was not the hierarchical way of other lands or churches. The religious imagination that grew out of experience was an early form of praxis theology. That pragmatism has continued to affect how Americans do theology, liturgy, and any other discipline.

The symbolic pioneers, the explorers, the reluctant, and the settlers, had their corollaries in religious imagination. The future of

25. Peter Fink, "The Challenge of God's Koinonia," *Worship* 59:5 (September 1985) 394.

the Christian memory would be differently interpreted by each group. For the explorers the present and future ought to be the base for structures that facilitate the dreams and visions of what can be. For the reluctant, only the past structures can maintain order and truth. If these do not contain the experience, then the experience should be changed, reinterpreted, or denied. For the settlers, past structures are a link to stability, but when the dream suggests other means of facilitation, these ought to be tried.

In the present stage of the new heavens and the new earth, the source of creating the contours of the dream is founded in the communal celebration of the Christian memory. Though there is a universality to the paschal mystery, the intimacy of the infinite is best experienced in communities where there is a sense of relationship and personal value.

The movement toward base communities and toward domestic churches may seem new, but it is quite old. Whether the churches will adapt older world views to incorporate newer realities remains hidden in the future of the memory. A radical and large scale evolution must take place in the decades ahead. Greater freedom on the part of local communities to formulate appropriate liturgies will be of immense help. But, ultimately, education of liturgical understanding and sensitivity, and translating that understanding into appropriate celebrations for particular communities, is more essential.

The liturgical reform is only beginning. There is still much that can and will be incorporated into the contours of the memory. Indigenization has only begun in the North American church. The religious imagination of a people committed to a new heaven and a new earth will keep the Christian memory alive and well. The future of the tradition is in the hands of those who celebrate the memory, who envision better structures to mediate that memory, and who hopefully continue to go forward until the Lord comes.

Further Thematic Development

1. The U.S. Bishops' Committee on the Liturgy issues a newsletter which is a useful summation of current liturgical issues and directives or correctives. Identify the major topics identified in the newsletter for the past five years, and critique the issues in light of the Notre Dame Parish Study of Catholic Parish Life. Phase III of

this study, "Pastoral Interpretations and Applications," will be in process through 1988. *The Parish in Transition* (Washington, D.C.: USCC, 1986), proceedings of a conference on "The American Catholic Parish in Transition," uses data from phase I and phase II of the study. Reports of the study are also available from: University of Notre Dame, Memorial Library, Room 1201, Notre Dame, IN 46556. Another descriptive source with pastoral reflections is Mark Searle, "The Notre Dame Study of Catholic Parish Life," *Worship* 60:4 (July 1986), pp. 312-33.

2. Review the basic issues covered in *Worship* and *Liturgy* over the past five years. How do the issues of concern and the approaches to these issues compare to each other, and to the items identified in *BCL Newsletter* mentioned in number one?

3. Construct a list of the available works on family spirituality or domestic liturgy that you have readily available in your own parish, college, university, or seminary library. As a group, research possible additions to the collection through publishing houses, diocesan and national liturgical centers.

4. Construct the contours of a liturgy that you feel expresses the spirit of the various communities to which you belong. Evaluate the different uses of space, time, readings, music, silence, and other symbols of the Christian memory that call the particular community into the future of God and the future of the world.

NINE

HOUSE CHURCH:
YESTERDAY, TODAY, TOMORROW

You may be led where you may not wish to go
(Jn 21:18)

FOR CHRISTIANS LITURGY IS THE LOVING EMBRACE OF ALL PEOPLE BY JESUS
Christ.[1] Liturgical spirituality is the Christian community's response to this transforming embrace. Liturgical spirituality is integral in its creativity, for there is one eschatological memory that
transforms and challenges the ecclesia of every age. Liturgical
spirituality is creative in its integrity because the imagination of
God for the world manifest in Christ Jesus calls forth from the
storeroom of possibility things new and old.

The universality of liturgical spirituality is experienced through
its incarnation in living and particular communities of memory.
The domestic church is such a particular community of memory.
The domestic church is an intentional, relatively permanent, and
highly participative ecclesia. The strength of its communal bonding is manifest in its conscious outreach to further communion in
the world. A sense of baptismal responsibility, manifest in shared

---

1. Karl Rahner, "Consideration on the Active Role of the Person in the
Sacramental Event," *Theological Investigations*, vol. 14 (New York: Seabury, 1976) 169-70.

vision and hope, provides a foundation for meaningful and challenging celebration of the Lord's Supper.[2]

If liturgical spirituality is the response of the Christian community to the cosmic embrace of Jesus Christ, domestic spirituality is the particularized response of the community to further the new creation in their circumstances. The mission of being and becoming evangelical is challenged, enlightened, and renewed at the cultic celebration of the Lord's Supper.

The increasing number of domestic churches throughout the world today raises both possibilities and perils for liturgical life and the cultic expression of that life. This chapter will focus three perspectives that contribute to the dialogue over possibilities and perils domestic churches raise for liturgical life today and tomorrow. First, the creative integrity of the domestic spirituality of early Christian households of faith will be summarized. Second, the integral creativity and liturgical spirituality of some twentieth century households of faith will be described. Third, the interdependence of basic ecclesial-liturgical issues will be addressed as well as some culturally specific issues for domestic churches of North America.

CREATIVE INTEGRITY: DOMESTIC SPIRITUALITY OF THE EARLY HOUSE CHURCHES

The social context of early Christianity included many forms of intentional human communities. Collegia, household units, and religious groups were three forms of intentional communities. Collegia included workers of different social status who shared the same talents and profession. The household unit was a familial, social, and political unit. The religious groups of Judaism and Hellenism were spontaneous groupings of persons who shared religious visions.

Paul's households of faith included these three structures of intentional communities. However, these communities were unique in the source, the composition, the meaning, and the expectations of community in the Lord Jesus Christ. The new crea-

2. Bernard Lee and Michael Cowan characterize domestic churches with the realities of koinonia, diakonia, leitourgia, and kerygma in *Dangerous Memories* (Kansas City: Sheed and Ward, 1986) 24-30.

tion in Christ demanded a constant challenging and transforming of the former interiorized socioreligious patterns. The dangerous memory of the Lord's Supper was a constant call to remember the ideal communion and to further it within the community and within the world.

Paul's missionary practice was to convert entire households and then to use these households as bases for further missionary activity. From the letters of Paul it appears that these domestic communities continued to meet in the homes of some of the members of the community (Acts 16:15, 31ff; 17:6; 18:1-8; Rom 16:3ff; 1 Cor 1:14-16; 11:19; Phil 2). Converts associated themselves with a household church. This community in turn was responsible for the initiation and formation of the convert. As the Christian community grew in size, the household character of ecclesia was retained through formation of other churches. The practice reflects the emphasis the early church put on strong communal bonding. These bonds were considered crucial in encouraging and safeguarding the quality of life expected of Christians.[3]

There could be many domestic churches in the same locale. These churches could originate in the household unit, the collegia unit, or the religious unit. This plurality of ecclesiae was still considered to be one church. Paul addresses one letter to the variety of churches, namely, Rome, Corinth. When Paul uses the term church, it is clear that these communities differ from other spontaneous associations of the time.

First, the churches do not belong to the people who are the members, nor to the district in which they are located. Paul's churches belong to the One who has called the community into being (1 Cor 1:1; 2 Cor 1:1; 1 Cor 10:32, 11:22; Rom 16:16). Second, the belonging is also a becoming. There is frequent celebration of the source of and possibilities for the community. Weekly celebrations of the Lord's Supper seem probable, but whether this is on Saturday night, Sunday morning, or Sunday night cannot be easily detected. Whether the domestic churches of a district ever met as a whole is also difficult to determine. Justin remarks that

3. Abraham J. Malherbe, *Social Aspects of Early Christianity* (Baton Rouge: Louisiana State Univ. Press, 1977) 86-91.

this still did not occur in his time.[4] Finally, there was a networking of these ecclesiae due to the mobility of the times. Both wealthy people and trades people were mobile. Paul and his co-workers are not characterized by any stability of location. Like Paul, Aquila and Prisca are at Pontus, Corinth, Ephesus, and Rome (Acts 18:1-3; 1 Cor 16:19; Rom 16:3ff.).[5] This mobility was responsible for the spread of creativity and integrity but it also contributed to controversies between the churches. Cultural, social, and prior religious imagination caused diversity. Unity in the midst of diversity required consistent reflection upon the freedom for which Christ set Christians free. As the ideal freedom of the new creation in Christ filtered through cultural and religious biases, Paul had to constantly remind Christians about the new creation. A familiar example of this is the corrective given to the Corinthian community.

The social stratification of society, reflected in the language and religious imagination of 1 Cor 11, was not easily overcome. Paul needed to remind the Corinthian community that the Lord's meal belongs to all, not just to the selected few who probably brought most of the food. The eschatological drama in which the just will be separated from the unjust is placed in the judgment situation of 1 Cor 11:29-32. Paul repeats the words of institution to confirm the mystery (1 Cor 11:23ff.).[6] It is significant that Paul does not direct criticisms against the community for attitudes toward bread and wine, toward God or toward Jesus Christ. Rather, the wine shared at the end of the meal, an eschatological anticipation of the communion of the kingdom, becomes a focal symbol. To drink this cup is to affirm the kingdom community on earth. Those who consciously distinguish strata in the community are not drinking the wine of the kingdom but a wine of judgment.[7]

Integration into the new family of God was reflected in the living acceptance and practice of the new meanings of brother and

4. Robert Banks, *Paul's Idea of Community: The Early House Churches in Their Historical Setting* (Grand Rapids: Eerdmans, 1982) 33-42. Banks cites Justin's First Apology, 67, to affirm the inadequacy of the supposition that all Christians met as one on Sunday.
5. Earle E. Ellis, "Paul and His Co-Workers," *New Testament Studies* XVII:3 (July 1971) 437-52.
6. Malherbe, *Social Aspects* 76-91.
7. Banks, *Paul's Idea of Community* 85-90.

sister. Though pagan clubs as well as religious groupings used the terms "brother" and "sister" to name their membership, the baptismal language of Paul expands the meaning. The new family of God expands familial horizons to universal proportions revealed in the paschal mystery. "Putting on Christ" means to renounce all divisions that favor some at the expense of others. Allusions to the language of the baptismal ritual proclaim this ideal (Gal 3:28, 1 Cor 12:13, Col 3:11).[8]

One context for Paul's baptismal language is the Judaic tradition of the Adam legends. These legends of Adam spoke of God's image as a "garment of light" with which the first human was clothed (Gen 1:26). This "garment of light" was lost when the human sinned and became divided. The separation of Adam from Eve represented the loss of the "garment of light," the original unity of "God's image" (Gen 2:21ff.). Once the separation occurred, "garments of skin," the human body as male and female, replaced the "garment of light" (Gen 3:21). So the two had to become one.

When anyone was baptized, the stripping of clothing represented the "stripping away" of the body of flesh or the "garments of skin" (Col 2:11). The reclothing symbolized the "putting on" Christ, "the garment of light." Baptismal commitment to be and to further the new creation in Christ meant furthering mutuality, equality, and communion proper to the new creation. How could the world put on Christ, the garment of light, when the Christian community still lived with the structural antinomies of male and female, Jew and Greek, slave and free, rich and poor?[9]

In the midst of this baptismal theology of internal and external communion, there remains an interesting mix of structure and anti-structure in the Pauline communities. Anti-structure is clear in the reflections about the Spirit who freely gives gifts to everyone for building the Body in love. The lists of charismata of word and deed are both freely given and open-ended (Rom 12; 1 Cor 12). Different communities have needs for different gifts, so the lists vary. Yet Paul orders the use of the gifts in the context of the

8. Wayne A. Meeks, *The First Urban Christians* (New Haven: Yale, 1983) 80-86.
9. Wayne A. Meeks, "The Image of the Androgyne: Some Uses of a Symbol in Earliest Christianity," *History of Religions*, vol. 13, 165-208.

socio-religious milieu of the community. Structure in the Pauline communities is a function of prudence, not of any command from the Lord or "hierarchy of gifts." Who could use which gifts, where, and when, varies with the community. Two examples can illustrate this.

In Rome and Macedonia Paul used women as well as men as his "co-workers." Culturally, women and men in these places would be acceptable as religious workers, singly or as a couple. First century Judaism did not allow women missionaries, an issue that Paul deals with flexibly and prudently.[10] In areas where both women and men functioned as synagogue leaders, collegia leaders, or household leaders, both men and women functioned as leaders of house churches. In Christian communities the leaders of the house churches also presided at eucharist. There is no historical grounds for assuming women did not do this.[11]

In Corinth, on the other hand, Paul raises some injunctions (1 Cor 11:2-26; 1 Cor 14:33-36). Even if the latter is post-Pauline, representing the patriarchal captivity of the new creation, two factors have conditioned the content. In Corinth the Isis cultic practices had formative effects upon many Christians, former practicers of the Isis cult. In Corinth there was also a strong Jewish cult, whose practices of uncleanness had an effect upon Judaeo-Christians. How do these practices illumine the texts of injunction?

In the cultic practices honoring the goddess Isis, women in prophetic ecstasy shouted out magical incantations and then let their hair down to effect their magical incantations.[12] In Jewish cultic practice (Lev 13:45, Nm 5:18) women let their hair down as a symbol of uncleanness. To avoid symbolic confusion in the Corinthian community, Paul insists that women keep their hair up (or

10. Banks, *Paul's Idea of Community* 150-60; Elizabeth Schüssler-Fiorenza, "Women in the Early Christian Movement," in *Womenspirit Rising,* ed. Judith Plaskow (New York: Harper and Row,1979) 84-92.
11. Herve-Marie Legrand, "The Presidency of the Eucharist according to the Ancient Tradition," *Worship* 53:5 (September 1979) 413-38; Elisabeth Schüssler-Fiorenza, *In Memory of Her* (New York: Crossroads, 1984) 168-84.
12. An extensive study of symbolic shifts of imagination from female goddess cults to male god cults, with the effects upon differences in male and female roles in the cultic practices, can be found in Gerda Lerner, *The Creation of Patriarchy* (New York: Oxford, 1986) 152-98.

cover their heads), remain silent, and that order be observed in assemblies. At the same time, Paul affirms equality in Christ, and the freedom of the Spirit to give gifts to all. However, the use of any gift is a matter of prudence, not a "revelation from the Lord."[13]

What can be concluded about the liturgical spirituality of these early households of faith? First, the cosmic reconciliation of the world in Christ is experienced in the creative integrity of a community that is one church in the one Lord, and living one baptismal responsibility. Oneness is not diminished by plurality of structures and practices. Second, the centrality of the Lord's Supper as formative, expressive, and critical of the communion of the new creation is essential to the evangelical essence of the community. Third, the communion manifest in the Lord's Supper extends beyond the celebrating community to an embrace of the world. Fourth, the freedom of the Spirit to give whatever gifts are necessary for the community is presumed. Different gifts of word and deed are given to different communities, and the list is an open-ended one. No gift was sacralized, for all gifts contributed to the new creation, a creation whose possibilities could not be envisioned. Fifth, a plurality of structures, of ministries, of use of gifts, and of rules of order emerged as a function of cultural and religious differences. Prudence appropriate for the particularity of the communities was manifest, though this was not confused with a revelation from the Lord.

Dramatic social-ecclesial evolution marks the distance between the early centuries and the twentieth century. However, this does not negate all similarities. The same Spirit speaks to the churches of the new creation in every age, in spite of the great dissimilarities of culturally conditioned hearing. The next section will describe the international rise of domestic churches in the twentieth century, and focus some of the similarities that are congruent with the earlier tradition.

Integral Creativity: Twentieth Century Households of Faith

The rise of domestic churches in the twentieth century represents a renewal of communal imagination which in many cases is a response to a lack of ordained priests. The particular history

13. Schüssler-Fiorenza, *In Memory of Her* 224-29.

and names for the domestic churches differs from country to country. Future vision, link to institutional leadership, possibility of eucharist, frequency of communal prayer, communal gatherings for reflection, and the manner of networking differ. However, the phenomenon of the domestic church shares the similarities of strong communal bonding, baptismal responsibility for furthering the new creation of justice and peace, the facilitation of gifts of the Spirit, and liturgical (or paraliturgical) celebrations of the Lord's Supper as essential to the community's life. A brief overview can demonstrate some of the plurality as well as the unity.

Brazil is a country with a relatively long experience of house churches. At the present time there are between eighty and one hundred thousand households of faith. This large number represents the results of community evangelization begun in the late 1950s as the number of clergy was declining. Assessing the movements among the people, the Brazilian bishops designed a pastoral plan for guiding the renewal experiences. Strong support came from the Medellin Conference of Latin American Bishops in 1968.[14]

A felt responsibility for the transformation of the church and of society has characterized the movement in Brazil. The context of liberation theology has provided the theological basis for communal visions of—and actions for—justice in the church and in the surrounding communities. Five major conferences of domestic churches have already been held. The union of the institutional church and the community of domestic churches is a positive sign for the renewal possibilities that lie ahead.[15]

Africa has also experienced the rise of households of faith. The number of domestic churches varies with geographic locale. In 1976 a plenary conference of bishops in Eastern Africa made the building of households of faith a pastoral priority for eighty-two dioceses. Over ten thousand communities have developed in Eastern Africa. In a 1976 synod Central African bishops made a five-year plan for building domestic communities. Bishops of

14. The conclusions of this conference are published as *The Present Day Transformation of Latin America in Light of the Council and Puebla: Evangelization at Present and in the Future of Latin America* (Washington, D.C.: National Conference of Catholic Bishops, 1979).
15. *Pro Mundi Vita* 43 (1985) 1, 2-6.

Upper Volta made intentional communities their focus at a 1976 Easter meeting. For a variety of reasons South African bishops have not moved as quickly in guiding the phenomenon.[16]

In the Philippines bishops of seventy-five dioceses have named the intentional community movement as a top priority for pastoral planning. The varieties of the communities in the Philippines represent great diversity. The composition of the groups range from conservatives, who wish to nourish private spirituality, to liberals who are passionately concerned for social justice.[17] Communities select their own leaders, who in turn receive systematic formation before they are officially installed as leader or minister. Communities gather weekly for prayer and again on Sunday for a liturgy of the word and communion service. The leaders gather monthly to share information so that there is some networking of churches. Twice a year all gather for learning sessions, reflection, and discussion. Priests preside at eucharist approximately five times each year.[18]

Households of faith in Europe represent a great diversity of composition, structure, mission, and relationship to the institutional church. Communities in Belgium, Holland, Germany, Italy, and Switzerland are in touch with the hierarchy, though there is no pastoral plan for guidance. The communities in Spain are condemned by some bishops and encouraged by others.[19]

In 1979 North American households of faith numbered about fifteen thousand.[20] Domestic churches in North America have not originated out of any one source. The communal bonding, shared vision, and a felt responsibility for mission may have begun in some form of renewal group like Cursillo, Marriage Encounter, Renew, or other communal experience. Members of the house churches tend to be articulate, better educated, white, and middle

16. *Pro Mundi Vita* 41 (1983) 3, 5-9.
17. *Pro Mundi Vita* 42 (1984) 4, 9-11.
18. *Pro Mundi Vita* 45 (1985) 3, 14-18.
19. *Pro Mundi Vita* 38 (1983) 4, 3-4. Cardinal Tarancon of Madrid strongly encourages reflection of what the Spirit is saying through the communities. Bishop Herras of Almeria has abolished intentional communities for being too independent of the hierarchy.
20. The estimate comes from a Woodstock Study published as *Tracing the Spirit*, ed. James Hug (New York: Paulist Press, 1983).

class. They are drawn to a vision and mission of empowering others, especially the poor, the marginal, and women. Unequal or hierarchical distribution of power that does not emerge from group identification of charisms makes them uneasy. There is a unity in the basic concern for social transformation that will further the dignity and equality of all people.[21]

The domestic churches of the twentieth century reflect the five characteristics of the early households of faith. First, there is the experience of being one church in one Lord, with one faith, one baptism, and one table of remembrance. Structures for the particular communities vary as they did in the early church. Unlike early church experience, relationship to the institutional church varies. Second, the centrality of the Lord's Supper is as essential to—and dangerous for—the life of the community as it was in the beginning. Unlike early church experience, there is a plurality of frequency and possibility for sacramental celebration of the eucharist. Third, the cosmic embrace of Jesus Christ for the world is both a judgment and a challenge for any lesser self-enclosed embrace. Fourth, respect for the diversity of gifts of the Spirit and their open-ended possibilities effect a highly participative structure relative to the nature of the domestic church and its mission. Unlike the early church, there are some presumed revelations of the Lord that override prudence in assessing who can do what with the gifts. Finally, there are culturally conditioned pluralities that exist as well as ecclesially conditioned differences. The mode of relationship to the one church, forms and frequency of networking, variations in the manner of training leaders, facilitating community gifts, the possibility and frequency of eucharist, and differences in the times of community gathering for prayer, reflection, and action are some of these pluralities.

The plurality and the unity experienced in the domestic church experience today suggests perils as well as possibilities for the future of the one church. A foundational issue is the relationship between ecclesia and eucharist. The possibilities of liturgical spirituality incarnate in and through domestic spirituality emerge from the resolution of this relationship. The next section will ad-

---

21. Bernard Lee and Michael Cowan have done an analysis of the North American experience in *Dangerous Memories*, pp. 61-111.

dress this basic issue with other possibilities that flow from its resolution.

LITURGICAL SPIRITUALITY, DOMESTIC SPIRITUALITY: POSSIBILITIES AND PERILS

Liturgical spirituality, the response of the Christian community to the cosmic embrace of Jesus Christ, is incarnate in the response of a particular community to the transforming power of that embrace. Domestic spirituality is a response to the liturgy of all life celebrated, centered, and transformed at the table of the Lord. Just as "the one and universal church does not manifest herself, nor has she any concrete existence, properly speaking, except in the local church," so is liturgical spirituality manifest through domestic spirituality.[22]

Domestic churches are fully "church," but no local church is wholly the church universal. Why? No particular church exhausts the wealth of the eschatological mystery of salvation. For this reason, every particular church, including Rome, must be open to a plurality of experiences of other particular churches. No local church can impose on other local churches a particular manner or pattern of being the church. If particular churches are wholly the church, their very constitution is sacramental. This means that sacramental celebration flows from its essence, being necessary for both the constitution and evolution of its being as church.[23]

This contemporary restatement of the essential, constitutive relationship between ecclesia and leitougia affirms what was clearly stated by Vatican II. "No Christian community, however, can be built up unless it has its basis and center in the celebration of the most holy eucharist."[24] This reflection is consistent with the tradition of relationship between community and eucharist set forth by Cyprian and Tertullian.

Cyprian goes so far as to say the community's right to the eu-

22. Louis Bouyer, *The Church of God,* trans. Charles Underhill Quinn (Chicago: Franciscan Herald Press, 1982) 396.
23. Leonardo Boff, *Ecclesiogenesis: The Base Communities Reinvent the Church* (New York: Orbis, 1986) 10-22.
24. "Decree on the Ministry and Life of Priests," 6; Abbott, *The Documents* 545.

charist is of divine origin.[25] Tertullian points out what ought to happen in the absence of a bishop or a college of presbyters.

> But where no college of ministers has been appointed, you the laity must celebrate the eucharist and baptize; in that case you are your own priests, for where two or three are gathered together, there is the church, even if these are lay people.[26]

The contrast of these early traditional positions with the position of the 1983 letter from the Congregation for the Doctrine of the Faith can be succinctly summarized.[27] The earlier tradition presumes there is no church without eucharist. The latter presumes desire is all that is necessary to receive the fruit of the sacrament. If this supposition is true for eucharist, then is it also true for presidency of the eucharist, for ordination to ministries, and for all other sacraments? The peril raised by the letter is focused clearly in the following observation.

> With an axiom taken out of context, the Congregation thus blithely disposes of God's dispensation to be among us . . . replacing God's desire to be among us in fleshly forms with a desire for the pseudo-sacral of the clerical order.[28]

The issue of the sacramental essence of the domestic church is an issue that can be transformative, reformative, or destructive of the sociological structures of the institutional church. Some possibilities were pointed out clearly seventeen years ago. On the one hand, "office-holders and clerics particularly are liable to become ecclesiological introverts. They think of the Church, not of the people."[29] On the other hand, the administrative unit of the

25. Cyprian, Epist. 67.4; 62.3; 73.7 cited by Edward Schillebeeckx, *Ministry: Leadership in the Community of Jesus Christ* (New York: Crossroads, 1980) n.5, 148.
26. Tertullian, De Exhort. Cast. 7.3, in Schillebeeckx, *Ministry* n.51, 153.
27. The statement appears in *Origins* 13:5 (September 22, 1983) 259–60.
28. David N. Power, "Liturgical Praxis: A New Consciousness at the Eye of Worship," *Worship* 61:4 (July 1987) 292.
29. Karl Rahner, *The Shape of the Church to Come* (New York: Seabury, 1972) 61.

parish is merely that, and not to be confused with the variety of possible manifestations of the church.

> When living Christian communities are formed by Christians themselves, when they possess and attain a certain structure, solidity, and permanence, they have just as much right as a territorial parish to be recognized as a basic element of the Church ... and to have its community leader recognized by the great Church through ordination.[30]

The ordination of the leader of a domestic church is one way to affirm the right of the community to the eucharist. Much of the theological discussion about the community's right to a priest is actually a discussion about the community's right to celebrate the eucharist.[31] The renewed consciousness of systemic injustice today situates this issue in that larger context with its liturgical ramifications. The justice of God revealed in Christ does not confuse ministry with possessive mastery.

> The Church is a servant of Christ and as such is not the owner but the steward of the eucharist ... In the eucharist, Christ's power is unleashed; it is a power over which the church has no control.[32]

Assuming that what the Spirit says to the churches is not under the control of an official church, what possibilities and perils are there for the domestic churches in the future? One scenario of possibility resides in the resolution of the relationship of particular churches to the church universal. If domestic churches are incarnations of the church universal, possibilities for authentic communal renewal and expression of liturgical life are many.

First, the strong bonding of domestic communities means that the engagement with life can be brought to worship in new ways. The respect for diversity of gifts as well as the sense of baptismal

30. Rahner, *Shape of the Church to Come* 109.
31. Edward Schillebeeckx, "The Christian Community and Its Office Bearers," Concilium 133, *The Right of the Community to a Priest*, ed. Edward Schillebeeckx and Johann Baptist Metz (New York: Seabury, 1980) 95-133.
32. R. Kevin Seasoltz, "Justice and Eucharist," *Worship* 58:6 (November 1984) 525.

equality of responsibility have effected highly participative structures. This in turn has facilitated the use of gifts without undue concern for gender, theological training, or the official affirmation of what gifts the Spirit can give to whom.

What may it mean for liturgical spirituality manifest in worship when a new sense of universality, community, and baptismal equality develops within a church still ordered by patriarchy? What will it mean if symbolization of the authentic presence of Jesus Christ among us is experienced in the communal breaking of bread and not in the insistence of reproductive gender sameness?[33]

> What kind of church will it be in which the pastoral care and anointing of the sick, the witnessing and blessing of Christian marriages, the reconciliation of sinners, the celebration of the eucharist, and the formation of new Christians are recognized as the right and responsibility of the whole community of the baptized?[34]

The concern of house churches for the bonding of community and respect for the gifts of the Spirit provides good ground for a response to the questions cited. As households of faith grow into the new creation for the world, more cosmic symbols and meanings of unity, healing, forgiving, reconciling, eating and drinking may globalize the horizons of Christian liturgies. Such enhancement of ritual tradition is more easily done in reflective domestic churches than in officially constituted ritual books composed for all churches of all nations.

The justice and liberation emphasis that characterizes the households of faith can open communal eyes and ears to the selectivity of God's word reflected in lectionary texts. This complex issue incorporates the imaging of God, the adequate inclusion of women as well as men as traditioners, the issue of the scriptures as idol or icon, and the universality of the new creation

33. Power, "Liturgical Praxis," *Worship* 61:4 (July 1987) 300.
34. Mary Collins, "Obstacles to Liturgical Creativity," Concilium 162, *Liturgy: A Creative Tradition,* ed. Mary Collins and David Power (New York: Seabury, 1983) 24.

reflected in the universality, inclusiveness, and complementarity of language.[35]

The megatrend culture provides North Americans with rather explicit cultural movements that provide a context for ecclesial-liturgical reflections as well. The megatrend culture suggests that centralized and top-heavy institutions cannot hope to move people forward if there is insistence on preserving structures that are non-participative.

> As our top-heavy centralized institutions die, we are rebuilding from the bottom up . . . The guiding principle of this participative democracy is that people must be part of the process of arriving at decisions that affect their lives.[36]

Any institution that seems to lack a long range vision of the future—emerging from present possibilities but also unpredictable possibilities—will not be credible to the informed person. There is need in a rapidly changing society to constantly reassess what business we are in. The American experience is that grass-roots movements, namely, civil rights, women's rights, consumer rights, and nuclear issues are ahead of any formal leaders advocating those rights.[37] The same may be said of organizations of church leaders.

In North American experience, hierarchies remain but their efficacy is gone. At the same time, the failure of hierarchies to solve problems forces people to talk to each other. Networks thrive when people are trying to change society. The way to effect change is to empower others, not to enforce power over others.

---

35. Mary Collins, "Naming God in Public Prayer," *Worship* 59:4 (July 1985) esp. 290-301; Robert Hurd, "Complementarity: A Proposal for Liturgical Language," *Worship* 61:5 (September 1987) 386-404; Marjorie Proctor-Smith, "Images of the Women in the Lectionary," Concilium 182, *Women: Invisible in Church and Theology*, ed. Mary Collins and Elisabeth Schüssler-Fiorenza (Edinburgh: Clark, 1985) 51-62; Marjorie Proctor-Smith, "Liturgical Anamnesis and Women's Memory: 'Something Missing'," *Worship* 61:5 (September 1987) 405-24; Gail Ramshaw, "De Divinis Nominibus: The Gender of God," *Worship* 56:2 (March 1982) 117-31.
36. John Naisbett, *Megatrends* (New York: Warner, 1984) 140, 175.
37. Naisbett, *Megatrends* 175-209.

"Networking empowers the individual and people in networks tend to nurture each other. Hierarchies promote moving up and getting ahead."[38]

Cultural contexts, for better and for worse, condition the imagination of the possible for ecclesial as well as cultural communities. If North American domestic churches can promote the bonding of persons that empowers each to reach out to others, the model may suggest a culturally pertinent revision of early households of faith. Just as the first century cultural milieu was conducive to particular experiences and expressions of the new creation, so is the present. The non-community experience, the individualism furthered by American independence, and the pursuit of loneliness all provide good ground for transforming communal experience.[39] Particularly the marginal, those who are ignored, rejected, or even suppressed by society and church, require ritualized communal gatherings. Such gatherings do occur, and they are ritualized, but often the rituals are officially ignored, occasionally suppressed, and seldom considered reformative of official rituals.[40]

If liturgical spirituality is a response to the cosmic embrace of the world in Jesus Christ, the domestic church may be in a better position to ritualize that life than the official church. Why? Domestic churches ritualize communal life as it is and ought to be. The universal church, represented through a minority committee, studies and then publishes ritual books which often represent a selective experience of the church universal. The rites may or

38. Naisbett, *Megatrends* 229.

39. Andrew Thompson, "Infant Baptism in the Light of the Human Sciences," *Baptism and Confirmation, Alternative Futures for Worship*, vol. 2 (Collegeville: The Liturgical Press, 1987) esp. 94-99.

40. Morton Kelsey, "Breakdown," *TheWay* 24:4 (October 1984) 287-95; Diane Neu, "Our Name is Church: The Experience of Catholic Christian Feminist Liturgies," *Concilium* 152 *Can We Always Celebrate the Eucharist?* ed. Mary Collins and David Power (New York: Seabury, 1982) 75-84; David N. Power, "Households of Faith in the Coming Church," *Worship* 57:3 (May 1983) 237-55; Rosemary Reuther, *Women—Church* (San Francisco: Harper and Row, 1985) 149-282; Sandra Schneiders, "Liturgy and Spirituality—the Widening Gap," *Spirituality Today* 38:3 (September 1978) 196-210; Starhawk, *The Spiritual Dance* (New York: Harper and Row, 1979).

may not embrace and enhance the prayer life of the church particular.

Ritual books presume a basic order, structure, and content of ecclesial prayer. Thus, a book like the Book of Blessing prioritizes who may normatively bless whom. Those who generically can hold no official position, namely women, are the last in the list. Officially, some women are pastoral associates or leaders of house churches, and many have theological and liturgical training. Yet, officially, an eight- or nine-year-old acolyte can liturgically "bless" a community before such a woman. The "blessing" theology of Jewish liturgical spirituality is clearly forgotten in such official expectations.

More importantly, if parish were not the presumed structure of the church, would a Book of Blessings be replaced by communal experience, liturgical education, and formative empowerment of all the baptized to bless? There is a need to question the presumptions of ecclesial and liturgical order manifest in the myriad debates over blessings, language fitting for the new creation in Christ, biblical translation debates that consistently confuse idols and icons. When domestic churches are told to desire the presence of the Lord rather than to incarnately obey the command of the Lord, there is need to clarify sacrament and sacrilege again.

Alternative communities of faith, the domestic churches, can be a source of renewed liturgical life and so of ecclesial life. Christian communities do not orient themselves to a future all worked out ahead of time, for no particular community—nor the church universal—shall exhaust the imagination of God for us. At the same time, Christians do have a responsibility to faithfully and intelligently work out how the kingdom of God can come in their time of history. Fear, lack of imagination that is far inferior to the surprise of the Spirit, and pseudo-sacral reasons for not engaging in the perils and possibilties of what the new creation calls forth obstruct the future of God. Ideally, Christians who image God must work to "create it (the future) in a spirit of unreserved commitment and hope, fashioning it by our own decision."[41]

Religious futurists perceive the task of religion in the twenty-first century to be that of a midwife who can facilitate birth of a

41. Karl Rahner, "Perspectives for the Future of the Church," *Theological Investigations,* vol. 12, *Confrontations* (New York: Seabury, 1974) 217.

new global community. As futurists know, thinking and hoping globally is manifest in reflecting and acting locally. Local experience of possibilities is the ultimate hope for global harmonic convergence. Whether religions can deal with their internal differences and look to the world beyond their self-concerned embrace is the issue at hand.[42]

The church who prays as it believes and believes as it prays is a church in constant need of further transformation. Liturgical life and the spirituality that is a response to—and somehow formative of—that life is in constant need of comparable transformation.

> If it is risky to play with sacred forms of public worship, it is probably riskier in the long run not to play with them . . . Playfulness evokes qualities of imagination without which life and love die of heaviness.[43]

At the same time, there is a sense of liturgical possibility that is sensitized and informed through a knowledge of the past as well as its possibilities for the future. What areas of critique ought to be brought both to the domestic churches and to the universal church in the matter of liturgical rituals (or paraliturgical rituals)?

First, how does the ritual relate to the history of its expression in context of the influences that affected its shape? Second, does the ritual continue to fulfill a prophetic function, that is, call the community into question? Third, is there an authentic use of symbols, a use that calls forth an openness to transcendence? Fourth, is the ritual an exercise in theological captivity, or in creative imagination that is freeing for an experience of the future of God?[44]

In a twentieth century megatrend society, the Christian dream of the kingdom of God is a dangerously creative memory. What if the new creation in Christ were taken seriously? What if liturgical

42. Earl Brewer, "A Religious Vision for the 21st Century," *The Futurist* XX:4 (July-August 1986) 14-18.
43. Bernard J. Lee, "Introduction to the Series," *Alternative Futures for Worship*, vol. 1, General Introduction, ed. Regis A. Duffy (Collegeville: The Liturgical Press, 1987) 22.
44. A context for these questions, and an elaboration of the meanings giving rise to the questions, can be found in David N. Power, "Unripe Grapes: The Critical Function of Liturgical Theology," *Worship* 52:5 (September 1978) pp. 386-99.

spirituality became formative, expressive, and creative of the shape of the church universal? What if the dream of the kingdom with no more divisions, no more structured pseudo-sacral roles in the community infected every community of the baptized? What if liturgical life on earth truly blessed all of life and became experientially an icon of the kingdom as it is in heaven?

What is essential is not the raising of these unanswerable questions. What is essential is the incarnate expression of at least partial but open-ended answers. This is the peril and the possibility that domestic churches can offer to the church universal.

> Where do we stand, on what ground, in what space?
> Remember, You wounded us with dreams—
> Can they be swept away like flying embers
> that keep the color of our days?
> Where do we stand,
> asking what questions, faced by what choice?
> We must take a beginning ... drink the stone cup ...
> —The Lord be with you.
> —And also with you.[45]

Further Thematic Development

1. Domestic churches have been the subject of many revised or alternative rituals in the Christian tradition. Study any of the following and critique these for the cosmic symbols and texts, the global nature of the prayer, the particular appeal to a specific group of people gathered for a particular purpose.

SOME SOURCES

Lee, Bernard, ed. *Alternative Futures for Worship* series, vols. 2-7 (Collegeville: Liturgical Press, 1987).
Reuther, Rosemary Radford, *Women—Church* (San Francisco: Harper and Row, 1985) esp. 122ff.

2. Family prayer and ritual life have become a focus for many as the earliest experience of "church." Consider any of the sources

45. Catherine de Vinck, "A Liturgy," *Cross Currents* XXIII (Fall 1973) 251-2.

for and ritualizing of prayer in the home. What values are furthered by these rituals? What adaptation of the rituals would be necessary to fit your own domestic experience?

SOME SOURCES

National Bulletin on Liturgy 12:68 (March-April 1979).
National Bulletin on Liturgy 14:80 (September-October 1981).
Hays, Ed. *Prayers for the Domestic Church* (Easton, Ks.: Forest of Peace Books, 1979); also *Prayers for the Servants of God.*
Huck, Gabe. *A Book of Family Prayer* (New York: Seabury, 1979).

INDEX

Liberty
  and American dream, 143-56
  and American spirit, 161-75
Liturgical prayer
  and house churches, 177-96
  and models of worship, 97-103,
    103-111, 120-35
  and Vatican II, 120-35
  expressive of life, 14-21, 78-84,
    130-35
  in Christian life, 14-19, 97-103,
    120-35
Liturgical spirituality
  and American experience, 150-56,
    161-74, 187-95
  and domestic churches, 177-96
  and Vatican II, 120-35
  as a school,
    7-9, 14-18, 19-20, 134-35
  Jewish, 23-46, 69-73
  reflections upon, 1-3, 7-12, 14-19,
    20, 187-95
Lord's Supper (see also Eucharist)
  and domestic churches, 177-96
  and new creation, 78-84, 131-33,
    161-74, 187-95
  and unity, 78-84, 130-131, 177-96
  clericalization of, 104-11, 120-25,
    127-30
  presidency, 99-103, 105-11, 120-25

Megatrends and liturgy, 187-95
Memory
  and holiness, 69-84, 130-31, 1
    33-35
  Christian, 69-70, 78-84, 130-31,
    133-35, 178-84
  Jewish, 23-46, 71-78
  North American, 139-57, 161-75,
    177-95
Metaphors of mutuality
  commandment, 25-28, 131
  food, 31-34, 71-78, 79-84
  halakha, 26-28, 47-50, 65
  kingdom, 47-50, 56-65, 79-84, 131,
    161-75
  Torah, 24-28, 38-41, 47-50

Ministries
  and charisms, 97-103, 125-27
  and house churches, 177-95
  and Vatican II, 125-27, 130-31
  clerical, 104-12, 120-25, 127-30
  lay, 54-55, 97-103, 125-27, 177-95
Model one, 104-12, 120-24, 126-29
Model two, 97-103, 129-30, 131-34
Models of spiritual direction
  liturgical, 7-9, 14-18, 133-35
  private, 12-14, 19-20
Models of worship
  and house churches, 177-95
  and world views, 97-112, 120-35
  operative in church history,
    97-112, 120-35, 177-95

New creation
  and American dream, 150-56,
    161-74, 177-95
  and American spirituality, 171-95
  and early Christians, 69, 78-84
  and house churches, 177-95
  and Paul, 96-103, 177-83
  and Vatican II, 120-35
  and world views, 96-112, 120-35

Office and order
  appointment, 106-11, 120-25,
    127-30
  community discernment, 96-103,
    177-95
  holy orders, 106-11, 112, 120-29,
    130-35
  in house churches, 177-83, 187-95
  in medieval church, 106-12
  in Psuedo-Dionysius, 106-9,
    120-25
Papal power, 109-10, 128-29, 120-21
Paschal mystery
  and Christian spirituality, 1-3,
    7-9, 14-17, 79-84, 131-35, 187-95
  and early church, 78-84, 96-103
  and house churches, 177-83,
    187-95
  and life direction, 1-3, 7-12, 19-20,
    134-35